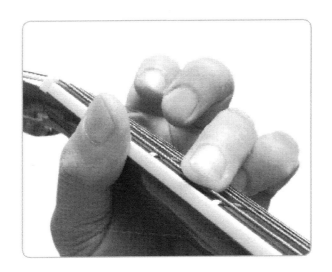

# THE
# ULTIMATE

# TEACH YOURSELF
# GUITAR BOOK

First Edition - 2014

Revised Editions - 2016 - 2018 - 2019

ISBN-13: 978-1499216356

ISBN-10: 1499216351

**Layout - Design & Photography**

Micaela Machado - Portugal
Emma Curtin - Ireland
PixelStudio - Bosnia

**Translations**

Marco Chu - Australia
Carlos Reyes - Mexico
Florica Dohan - Ireland
Jean-Michel GEORGE - France
Joana Peixoto Meneses - Portugal

HOMEGUITARACADEMY.COM

If this is your first day learning guitar you're in good company. All the greats had a first day too - and began a lifetime playing guitar that day.

YOU CAN BEGIN

A LIFETIME PLAYING GUITAR

TODAY!

# *YOU*
# *WILL LEARN*

- TO STRUM IN PERFECT TIME

- THE MOST PLAYED RHYTHMS

- THE MOST PLAYED CHORDS

- TO CHANGE CHORDS FAST

- TO IMPROVE SOUND

- TO READ CHORD BOXES

- TO READ GUITAR TABLATURE

*AND MUCH MORE!*

# CONTENTS

# HOW TO LEARN GUITAR

The ability to play guitar is *A Priceless Gift*. It lets your heart speak, and your imagination roam. Even when words fail, music speaks. And yet, unlike material wealth, once you have it, no one can take it away from you.

The lessons in this book have helped thousands of people to play guitar. They are the most *Complete, Individual and Personalised* you will ever find. You start simply by knowing what not to do - and also by making sure you have the right guitar to learn on.

From there, it is vital that you follow each lesson step by step. Don't just read them. Personalise them. Interact with the thumb, finger, and bar chord techniques. Highlight tips that really transform your guitar playing.

## MAKE THIS YOUR OWN BOOK

Do not skip lessons. The only way they will not work is if you're too eager to move to the next lesson.

By taking the time to absorb what you just learned, the quality of your guitar playing will be so much better.

Most importantly, all your practice is pre-planned from start to finish. You know exactly what to work on and won't forget to practice anything.

As well as being *The Key To Your Success*, the "Practice Programs" keep you on track from start to finish. And you can achieve in a few weeks, what took many people years to learn.

*So Come On Now ... Pick Up Your Guitar* ... and come with me on *A Truly Unique Musical Journey.*

# LESSON 1

HOW NOT TO PLAY GUITAR

START AT PERFECT

HOW TO POSITION
YOUR CHORD HAND

HOW TO READ CHORD BOXES

20 EASY GUITAR CHORDS
THAT SOUND AMAZING

# HOW NOT TO PLAY GUITAR

There are *9 Reasons Why People Fail* to learn guitar. Avoid them and you have just about written your own guarantee of success. Here they are;

1   Weak fingers

2   Bad guitar teachers

3   Bad thumb positioning

4   Learning music theory

5   Learning rhythms badly

6   Learning G the wrong way

7   Holding a guitar pick badly

8   Learning on nylon string guitars

9   Holding guitar neck in chord hand

## BAD HOLD

With a bad grip you can play basic rhythms but you will find advanced rhythms very difficult to perfect.

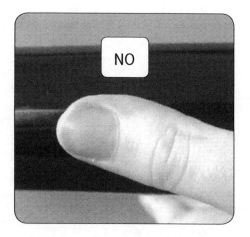

## BAD THUMB

If your thumb is badly positioned, fast chord changing is impossible.

Also your guitar will produce a muddy sound at the start of any chord you play.

Your thumb is positioned before or at the same time as your fingers. *NEVER AFTER THEM*. This has a huge impact on how your hand moves up and down the guitar.

Many people leave it behind or raise the knuckle. *This Is Fatal*. If your thumb falls sideways you can play basic chords but you will not be able to change quickly from one chord to another.

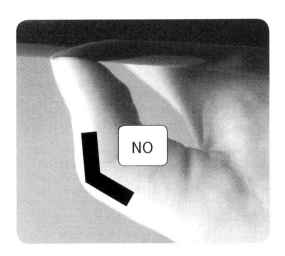

# RAISED THUMB KNUCKLE

This locks your fingers. You might be able to learn some chords from this position, but again, fast chord changing is impossible.

# THE GREATS
# CAN'T READ MUSIC
# WHY SHOULD YOU?

Did you ever buy a teach yourself guitar book...or enrol on a program of guitar lessons only to end up being taught music theory instead? So many people lose interest over this. *Sheet Music Is Not Music - It Is Ink On Paper.*

Also, sheet music does not show you how to set up, which fingers to use, or how to position your thumb and hands. All you need are guitar boxes and guitar tablature, which takes only five minutes to learn.

Learning the G chord as shown below is one of the main reasons why people give up playing guitar. This G only works when you pick each string one by one. But not when you strum all the strings at once.

*It Sounds Muddy*. And it can lead to other problems as you try to improve.

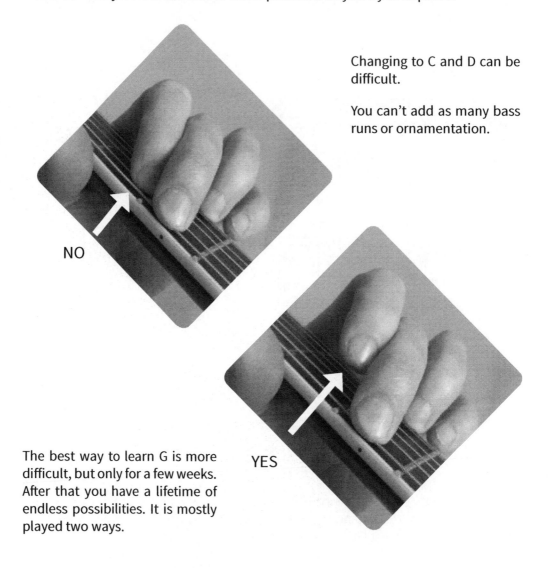

Changing to C and D can be difficult.

You can't add as many bass runs or ornamentation.

NO

YES

The best way to learn G is more difficult, but only for a few weeks. After that you have a lifetime of endless possibilities. It is mostly played two ways.

One gives a rich airy sound. The other frees your 1st and 2nd fingers to add more notes, polychords, and bass runs.

Most beginners pull the guitar neck back and crouch out and down to see the strings. Avoid this and you will learn and improve much much faster. And your guitar will be so much easier to play.

A faulty set up closes many doors

It also can block the air supply needed to sing well

# START AT PERFECT

How you set up to play guitar has a huge impact on how quickly you learn. Neglect this vital starting point and it's much more difficult to play. It only takes a few minutes to learn, but you greatly increase your chances of success.

Can you keep the guitar neck angled out *About The Length Of Your Forearm*. This sets your hand in front of you, the same as turning a key in a door. It makes chord changing much easier, and helps to release your natural ability.

# STRETCH YOUR HAND

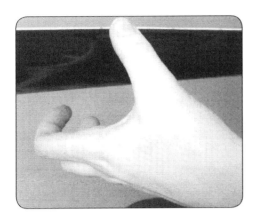

Stretching your hand helps you to **Power Down The Chords** to get good sound. Especially if you're a beginner or have small hands.

It also keeps your fingers close to the fretboard during chord changes.

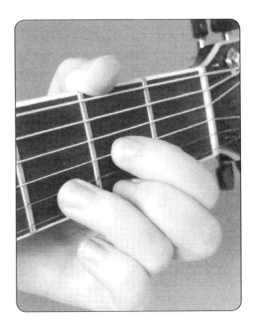

You do not stretch your rhythm hand. The correct feeling for playing guitar is a **Stretched Chord Hand** combined with a **Relaxed Rhythm Hand**.

# HOW TO POSITION YOUR CHORD HAND

Here is *One Of The Great Secrets* of playing guitar. In fact without it nothing is possible. From The Eagles to Elvis and from California to New Zealand you'll see *"The Guitar Triangle".*

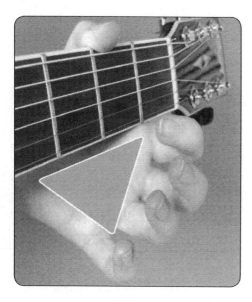

YES

If you watch any great guitarist in any style of music anywhere in the world you'll see *"The Guitar Triangle".*

Be very careful not to lose *The Triangle* while positioning your fingers.

You will also find it much easier and faster to change to most open chords if you maintain it during the chord change.

- Keeps fingers in front of guitar
- Makes room for fingers to move
- Lets you play with your fingertips
- Prevents knuckles from collapsing
- Makes chord changing easier

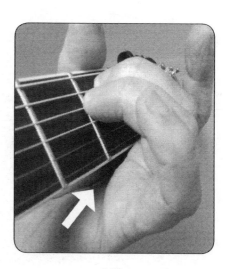

NO

To play most open chords on natural ability your *Fingers Are Set Horizontal* to the frets.

Practice this with great care. It should soon become easy and effortless.

You can also set your hand the same as *Holding A Flower*. Then seperate your thumb and first finger the width of a guitar neck.

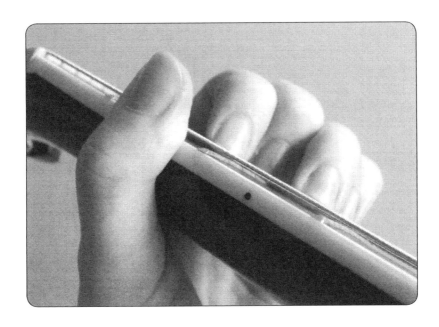

# HOW TO READ CHORD BOXES

Chord boxes are hugely helpful if you're an experienced guitarist. But because they only show you the front of the guitar neck, *They Do Not Work For Most Beginners*.

However, if you're a beginner the secret is to combine *The 3 Step Approach (Page 26)* with the chord box. Now they're *Much Easier To Follow* - and save you time.

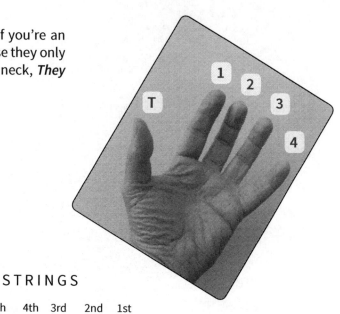

**STRINGS**

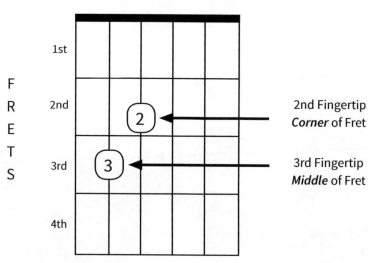

2nd Fingertip
*Corner* of Fret

3rd Fingertip
*Middle* of Fret

# 20

## EASY
## GUITAR CHORDS
## THAT SOUND AMAZING

Eм

A2

Dмaj9

Aм7

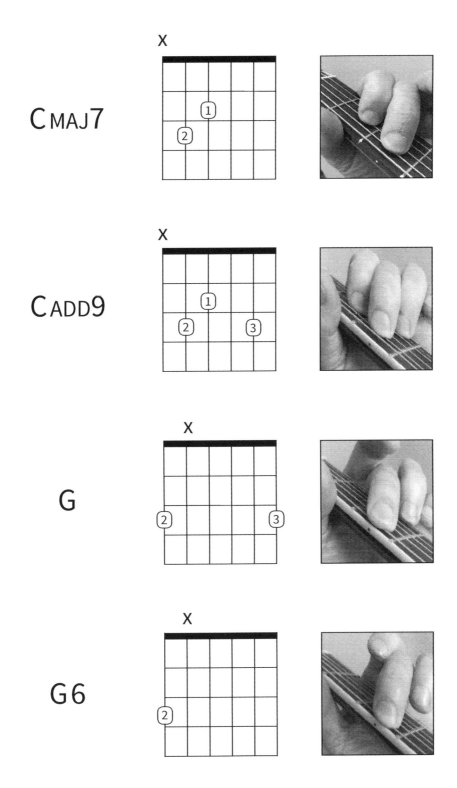

Cmaj7

Cadd9

G

G6

**Eᴍ7**

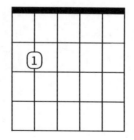

X

**Aᴍᴀᴊ7**

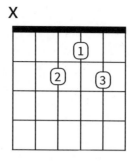

X  X

4ᴛʜ Fʀᴇᴛ

**Fᴍᴀᴊ7**

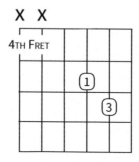

X

**D2**

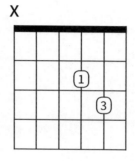

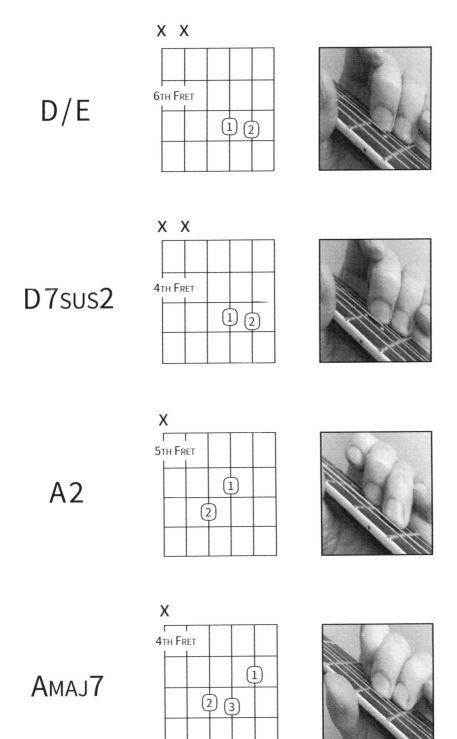

D/E

X X

6TH FRET

① ②

D7SUS2

X X

4TH FRET

① ②

A2

X

5TH FRET

①

②

AMAJ7

X

4TH FRET

①

② ③

**E7sus4**

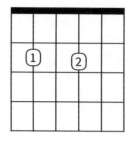 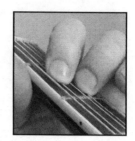

**E7**

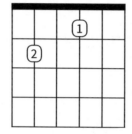 

**Gmaj7**

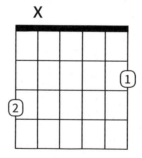 

**Dmaj7**

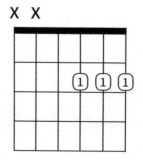 

# LESSON 2

THE BEST WAY TO LEARN CHORDS

THE BEST GUITAR FOR YOU

EVERYTHING YOU NEED

# THE BEST WAY TO LEARN CHORDS

The absolute best way to learn guitar chords is to

**1**  Tilt your guitar

**2**  Stretch your hand

**3**  Play the chord

From there, if you **Practice 2 Chords At A Time** you can also dramatically **Speed Up Your Chord Changes (the bit between them).** Whether you're a beginner or professional, D is D and G is G. But the professional is **Much Faster Between Chords**.

## *1*  *TILT* - YOUR GUITAR

Tilting makes learning chords **So Much Easier**. The guitar is now doing some of the work for you. It also helps to produce **A Good Sound**.

# 2 *STRETCH* - YOUR HAND

The
Guitar
Triangle

Page 16

# 3 *PLAY* - THE CHORD

The simple 3 step approach here is *Technically Perfect* and *Exactly As Played* by top guitarists.

It can help you achieve in weeks, what many people took years to learn.

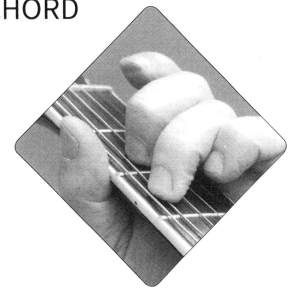

# THE BEST GUITAR
# FOR YOU

If you're a beginner you need to know if you strum better with your right or left hand. The one you write with is almost always the hand you strum a guitar with. If you're not sure try strumming a guitar both ways to see which is most natural.

Most professionals play *Slim Neck - Steel String - Acoustic Guitars. So Should You (unless you want to play classical guitar).*

They're much easier to play. Especially if you're a beginner or have small hands. And the fretboard is a the same as an electric guitar.

Once your fingertips harden, a steel string acoustic guitar sounds much better than a nylon string classical guitar.

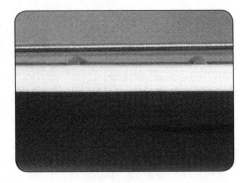

Steel Strings
Close To Fretboard

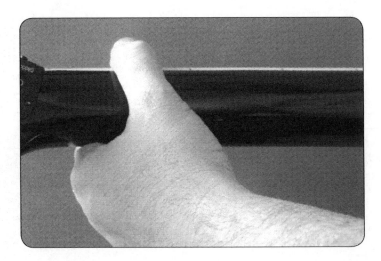

Slim Neck

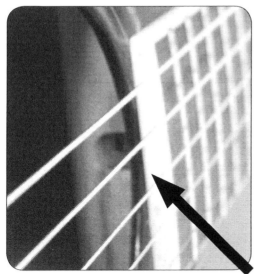

Light guage strings are easier to play and won't hurt your fingertips too much. By keeping a guitar in a case when not practicing the strings can last for a year or more.

If it's left out they tend to gather dust and need to be replaced often. You can also wipe them after playing.

Adjust
Guitar Neck

# GIRLS

Many of you have smaller body frames than men so it makes more sense to learn on a slim size and slim neck guitar.

As well as being much easier to play, you will be much more comfortable.

# EVERYTHING
# YOU NEED

Acoustic
Guitar Pick

Electric
Guitar Pick

Guitar Tuner

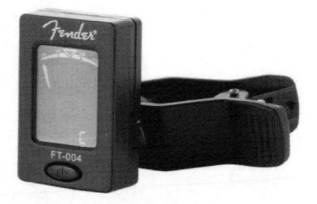

Clip-On
Guitar Tuner

If your guitar has a built-in tuner you do not need to buy one. A *Clip On Tuner* is the easiest to use, *Especially If You're A Beginner*.

String Winder

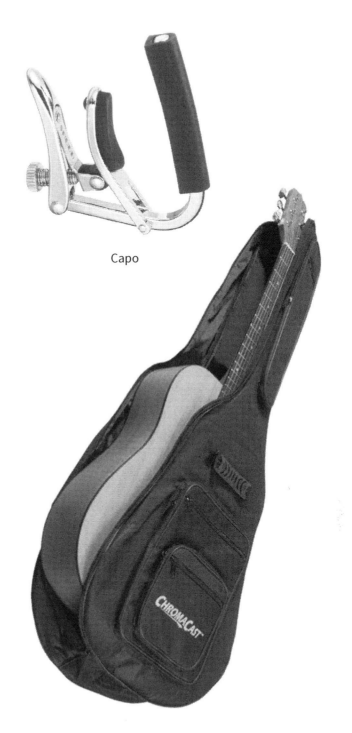

Capo

# GUITAR GIG BAG

Make sure the *Zip Runs Down The Side* from top to bottom.

It's so much easier to put your guitar into, and take it out of, this type of guitar bag. Also it's better if the bag is well padded.

# PRACTICE PROGRAM

# LESSON 2

- Practice A Good Set Up - *Page 14*

- How To Read Chord Boxes - *Page 18*

- Learn 2 New Chords - *Page 20 - 24*

- Reread How Not To Play Guitar - *Page 10*

---

# NOTES

# LESSON 3

How To Tune Your Guitar

How To Hold A Guitar Pick

How To Play Rhythm Guitar
Part 1

# HOW TO TUNE YOUR GUITAR

Guitar tuners can be tricky for beginners to use. Because they process sound waves you have to pick a string to bring it alive. Then you need to keep sounding the string to keep it responding....and turn the tuning head at the same time to tune the string.

6th String - *INSIDE* Tuning Head

A guitar tuner can process only one sound at a time. If it hears more it doesn't know which sound to process and gets confused.

A clip-on guitar tuner will solve all these problems instantly. They are the most user friendly of all tuners because they only work when attached to the guitar head.

So they hear your guitar and nothing else. You can even tune with it in very noisy or crowded areas.

A useful tip before learning to use a tuner is to start picking the 6th string and rest your thumb and finger on the inside tuning head. But don't turn it.

Then start picking the 5th string and move your thumb and finger out to the next tuning head. And go to the 4th string moving to the outside tuning head.

3rd String - *OUTSIDE* Tuning Head

When you go to the 3rd string you have to start on the bottom outside tuning head and work back in.

Many people go bottom inside tuning head and break a string. If you do this drill three times it gives you a good feel for using a tuner.

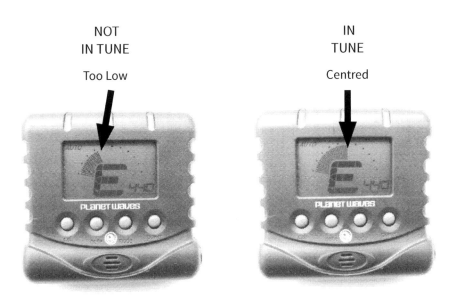

It's not enough to centre a needle or get a green light. The note on your tuner must match the string you are tuning. If you're using a tuner like the one shown here make sure there isn't a *# symbol* appearing on the top right corner of your screen.

Sometimes the strings need to be tuned more than once. After tuning it's a good idea to strum a little to settle them. Then tune them again and you're ready to play.

| 6th String | *E* | 3rd String | *G* |
| --- | --- | --- | --- |
| 5th String | *A* | 2nd String | *B* |
| 4th String | *D* | 1st String | *E* |

# HOW TO HOLD
# A GUITAR PICK

Some people don't like using a guitar pick. They say it slips as soon as they start playing.

But in reality it's their fingers that lose position because they're not holding it the right way. This exercise gives you a great way to hold a guitar pick.

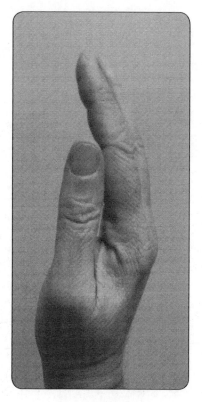

Reach Out As If
To Shake Hands

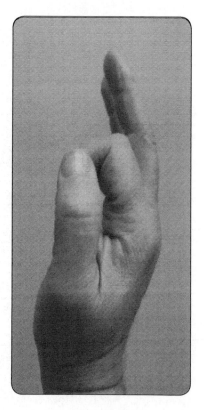

Then Hook
Your 1st Finger

# PLAYERS VIEW

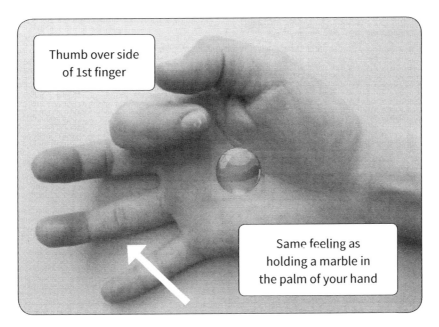

Thumb over side
of 1st finger

Same feeling as
holding a marble in
the palm of your hand

Curve And Separate These Three Fingers

## GRIP PRESSURE

On a scale of 1 to 10 - *About 3*

You can slide your thumb or the pick
a little for different sounds.

The ideal grip looks like the wing of
an aeroplane. For rhythm guitar use
about *Half* the pick. For lead guitar
about a *Quarter* or less.

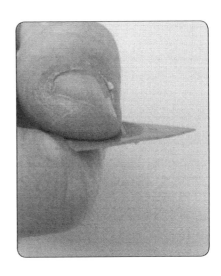

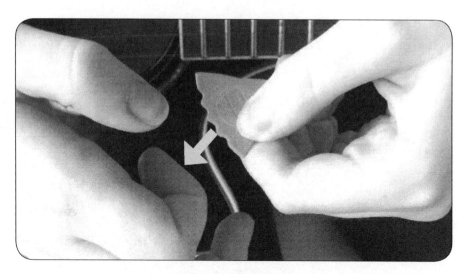

It's better to perfect the right hold with two hands

While learning this grip it's vital that you use two hands. Set your hand up and position the guitar pick with the other hand. Trying to do this with one hand can lead to problems. Once you have perfected a good grip it will be easy to do one handed.

It's very easy to lose a guitar pick. When finished playing, place the pick between the strings as shown here. And it will always be there when you want to play.

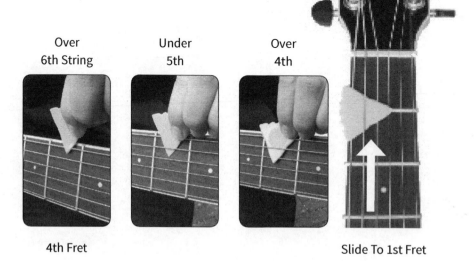

<table>
<tr><td>Over<br>6th String</td><td>Under<br>5th</td><td>Over<br>4th</td><td></td></tr>
<tr><td>4th Fret</td><td></td><td></td><td>Slide To 1st Fret</td></tr>
</table>

This style of pick sounds great on acoustic guitar. Not suitable for electric guitar.

This style of pick is ideal for electric guitar. Can be used on acoustic but more difficult to play with. Also does not sound as good as the one on left.

# HOW GUITAR
# CHORDS
# SOUND

A, D, G etc     HAPPY

Em, Am etc     SAD

A7, E7 etc     BLUES

Am7 etc     SAD / BLUES

Amaj7 etc     DREAMY

# HOW TO PLAY RHYTHM GUITAR

## *PART 1*

Top guitarists hold a pick with their thumb and fingers. *BUT THAT'S ALL*. They strum with their *Arm and Wrist*. It's a completely seperate action to holding a guitar pick.

## DOWNSTROKE

Plectrum Pointed
*Up*

Strumming from over the soundhole gives you a smoother sound. And because the strings seem to bend easier the pick is less lightly to slip.

Don't reach here with your arm. Instead angle the guitar neck out more. This resets your hand and arm without losing its natural playing position.

How well you strum a guitar depends on

- How good your set up is

- How well you hold a guitar pick

- Holding it at the right angle, and

- A combination of arm / wrist action

# UPSTROKE

Plectrum Pointed
*Down*

- *Downstroke* - 6 strings or less

- *Upstroke* - Mostly 3 or 4 strings

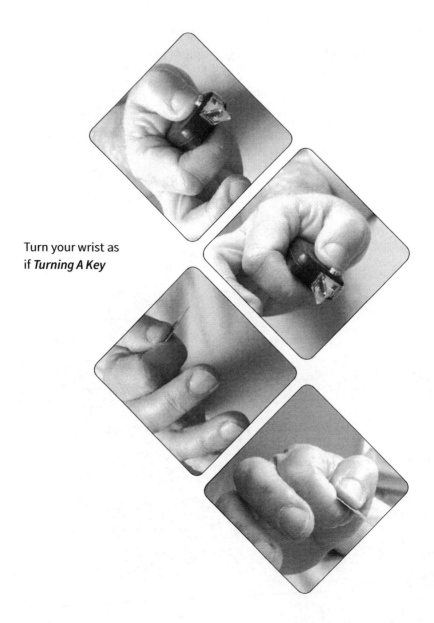

Turn your wrist as
if *Turning A Key*

Some guitarists don't use a pick at all. Instead they strum with their thumb (downstrokes) and 1st finger (upstrokes), or their first finger only for up and down strokes.

Others hardly ever use their fingers and prefer holding a guitar pick. By practicing each method you will gradually see your own playing style developing.

# LESSON 4

BEGINNERS GUITAR
FINGER EXERCISE

# 18
GUITAR SKILLS

# BEGINNERS FINGER EXERCISE

If you're a beginner *Your Fingertips Are Too Soft* to produce clear sound. It usually takes *About Three Weeks* for them to harden. Secondly you need four skilled fingers. This exercise will help you to quickly upskill and strengthen all your fingers.

Holding A Phone

Turning A Key

Holding A Glass

Holding A Spoon

In everyday life you use your thumb and first two fingers for most activities. The 3rd and 4th are seldom used except maybe for typing or playing a piano. Even then you're only lightly touching the keys. Pressing guitar strings is very demanding on all four of your fingers.

How often did you try to move one finger and a different one moved instead? This exercise will cure it. At the same time it gives you *18 Skills* that are in all guitar songs.

Practice it slowly and often at first. In a few days you will be amazed at how much easier it is to move your fingers independently of each other.

# WHAT THIS EXERCISE DOES FOR YOU

- Stretches thumb and back of your hand

- Strengthens the weaker fingers

- Makes fingers independent of each other

- Teaches you good thumb positioning

# STEP 1

- Your fingers approach from under the guitar neck.

- Then place all four *Fingertips* on the 6th string - one in each fret *(Page 46)*.

Once you have a good set up be very careful not to come out of it as you play. Remember Lesson 1? After setting up perfectly, you need to hold a very good set up position as you practice. It is actually much easier than trying to play from the crouched position.

1st Fingertip
*Corner*
*Of Fret*

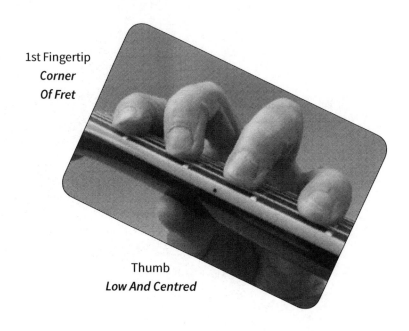

Thumb
*Low And Centred*

Too
Crouched

Elbow Out
Too Far

# STEP 2

- Move your *1st Fingertip* down to the 5th string 1st fret

- Now move your *2nd Fingertip* down to the 5th string 2nd fret, and so on

- It's vital that you *Move Only One Finger At A Time*

Now try to move your *3rd Fingertip* down a string without moving the others. Not so easy…is it? Because it's still too weak to play guitar. You might have to use your other hand to move it. Keep doing this exercise and it will start moving on its own.

# STEP 3

- Now move your *4th Fingertip* to the 5th string 4th fret

- Then you start with your 1st finger again down to the 4th string 1st fret and so on

*The Complete Exercise* is on the next two pages. Each time you do this exercise you're a step closer to playing guitar.

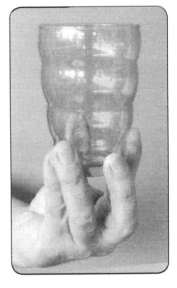

Very Similar To This
Natural Hand Position

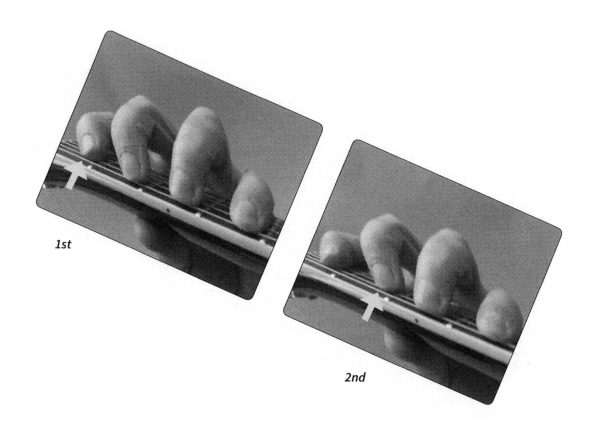

1st

2nd

# CRAMP

Do you feel cramp during this exercise? Don't worry. It's quite normal. Rest your hand until you feel ready to start again. Once your hand is strong it won't cramp anymore.

This exercise really exposes any weakness in your chord hand and fingers in relation to playing guitar. *But it's Also The Solution*.

- Once you arrive at the finish you can practice back up one finger at a time.

- Start with the 1st finger up one string, then the 2nd finger up one string, then the 3rd and so on.

- Keep going until all four fingers are back on the sixth string. You will find it much easier going back up.

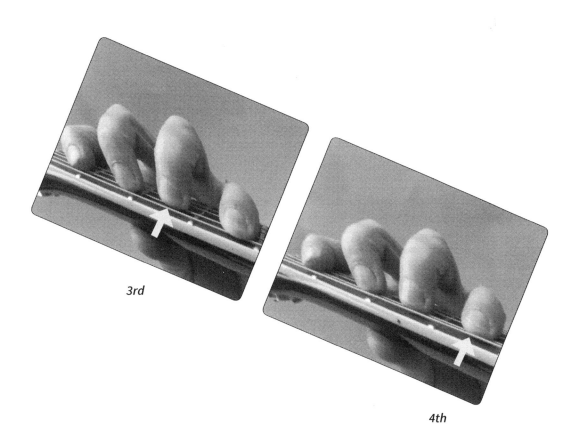

3rd

4th

# PRACTICE PROGRAM

# LESSON 4

- Practice A Good Set Up - *Page 14*

- Practice Finger Exercise - *Page 48*

- Make Sure You Are Not Crouched - *Page 46*

- Practice Strumming - *Page 40*

---

# NOTES

# LESSON 5

HOW TO PLAY RHYTHM GUITAR
PART 2

HOW TO IMPROVE SOUND

HOW TO PRACTICE

# HOW TO PLAY RHYTHM GUITAR
## PART 2

To strum on time you need to *Softly Roll Your Rhythms*. It is the great key to good sound and perfect timing. Even though there are thousands of different sounding rhythms, there is only one pattern for them all. *Here it is.*

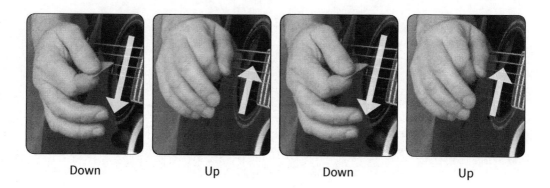

| Down | Up | Down | Up |

*GREY* Arrows - *Miss* The Strings

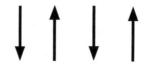

*BLACK* Arrows - *Strum* The Strings

Once a song starts can you feel how it rolls along? It doesn't start stop start stop. To do this on guitar your hand must have a down up down up non stop rolling movement.

In many guitar lessons, someone trying to teach you will say go down down down down. This is very misleading for many people. If I do four downstrokes in a row my hand will hit the ground.

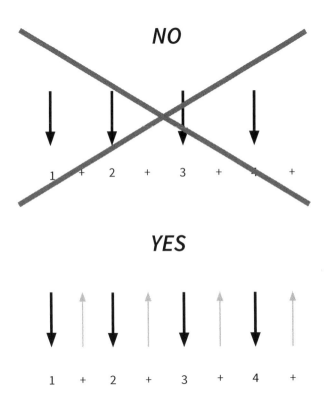

- To do four downstrokes
- You must also do upstrokes between them
- You continually roll your *Arm / Wrist* up and down
- But your audience only hears the black arrows

# HOW TO IMPROVE YOUR SOUND

For the first few weeks your fingertips are too soft to produce clear sound. It usually takes *About Three Weeks* for them to harden.

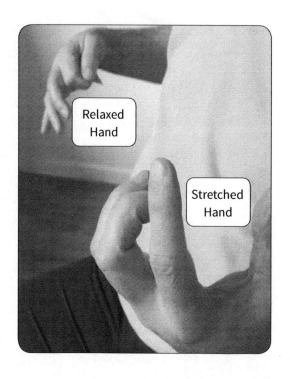

## IN THIS PICTURE

- My chord hand is *Stretched*

- My rhythm hand feels *Light*

- And I'm *Sitting Tall*

Because your fingertips have to press the strings harder than you thought, it causes your other hand to strum or pick too loud.

To produce pure sound, your chord hand is held firm and your rhythm hand is lighter and relaxed.

# FIRST STRING NOT SOUNDING

Many chords such as E, Am, and C have an open 1st string. Also your hand has a tendency to touch and mute the same string. For most chords with an open 1st string professionals leave a gap about the width of a small coin. They do this by *Dropping Their Wrist*.

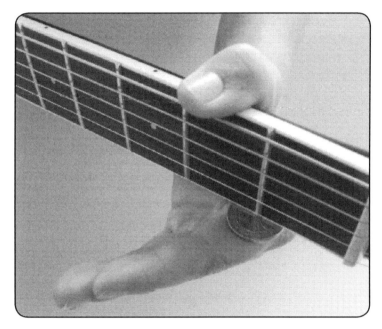

Practice With A Coin

Also beginners often find that a finger pressing the 2nd string is accidentally touching the 1st string. If that is you take the finger off the 2nd string and reposition your hand and fingers so that the 1st string now sounds.

Then put the finger back on. From here you should soon be able to finger the 2nd and also sound the 1st.

# HOW TO PRACTICE

Practice makes perfect. How many times have you heard that before? *But It's Not True*.

## PRACTICE DOES *NOT* MAKE PERFECT

To become a good guitarist quickly, only

## PERFECT PRACTICE
## MAKES PERFECT

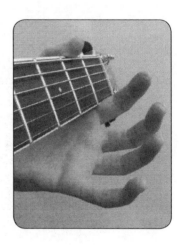

This approach is often the difference between success and failure.

Another reason why people fail is because they try to play songs from the start. In other words playing with two hands at the same time even though neither is upskilled enough.

A much easier and softer way would be to upskill each hand on its own. It may take longer but your chances of success are greatly increased, *Especially If You're An Adult*.

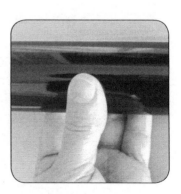

The best time to practice is *Just After You've Learned A New Technique*. While it's still fresh in your mind you capture it much quicker and easier.

# TAKE YOUR TIME

To build a house you need **A Solid Foundation**. To learn guitar well you also need a solid foundation.

Imagine building a house three floors high and this happens;

*Day 1*  You finish the ground floor

*Day 2*  You finish the first floor

*Day 3*  You are just about to finish the next floor and the whole house falls down.

# WHY?

The cement on each floor didn't get enough time to set. In other words **It Wasn't Aged**. Or you went to the next level too soon.

Learning guitar is the very same. **Your Pacing Has To Be Right**. Moving too fast might work for the basic skills but you will be found out once you move up a few levels.

If you practice the right way guitar playing comes to you in its own time.

# PRACTICE PROGRAM

# LESSON 5

- Practice Finger Exercise - *Page 48*
- Practice Strumming - *Page 40*
- Practice Rolling - *Page 52*
- Read How Not To Play Guitar - *Page 10*

---

# NOTES

# LESSON 6

How To Play Rhythm Guitar
Part 3

How To Play On Time

3 New Guitar Rhythms

# HOW TO PLAY
# RHYTHM GUITAR
## *PART 3*

Can you listen to a slow song that you know well? As it's playing pick up your guitar and mute the strings with your chord hand.

1    Count  1  2  3  4  1  2  3  4. If that does not work put on another slow song until you can clearly hear  1  2  3  4 1 2 3  4.

2    Start **Softly Strumming** the strings up and down until you are on time with the song.

Your chord hand keeps the strings muted while you are doing this. It's so much easier to strum when you don't have the added pressure of playing chords at the same time.

*Very Important*
A Good Hold

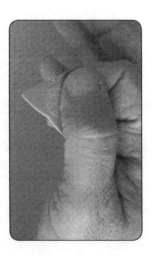

Eventually you should be able to find a rhythm to suit any song you want to play. It may not be exactly as recorded but the timing will be right. Also your own style will be starting to develop.

All songs can be played in single or double rhythm or a combination of the two. Here are three exercises that are a stepping stone to all guitar rhythms.

## EXERCISE 1  Played Slow & Fast

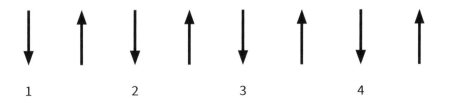

1       2       3       4

## EXERCISE 2  Played Fast

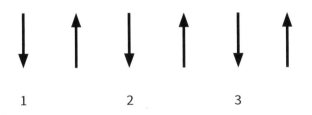

1       2       3

## EXERCISE 3  Played Slow & Fast

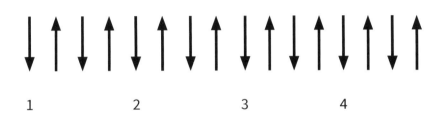

1       2       3       4

# HOW TO
# PLAY ON TIME

Counting and Foot Tapping are simply tools to correctly learn guitar rhythms. They help you to put *The Right Strum* in *The Right Place* at *The Right Time*. Once a rhythm is learned, *Stop Counting and Tapping*. You don't need them now. Just enjoy playing it.

As soon as you want to learn a new rhythm count and foot tap that rhythm until you have it. Again, once you have, no counting or tapping. Just enjoy playing it.

1   Can you listen to a slow song with a beat that is easy to follow?

2   Close your eyes and visualise yourself playing the song on guitar

3   As its playing count

1       2       3       4

Close Your Eyes

# FOOT TAPPING

Yes

The Best Way

Maybe

Foot tapping and playing guitar at the same time is not as easy as it looks. Most people have to practice it a lot and very slowly before they perfect it.

If you're a beginner you won't be able to strum on time with most songs. You will however be able to foot tap all of them.

By linking your strumming hand to your foot tapping you will soon strum guitar rhythms correctly. You will also be able to play with other musicians.

It's best to tap with the foot that's not under the guitar. The best way to tap is by lifting your foot completely off the ground when strumming.

It is more difficult than toe or heel tapping but the results are better. For rhythms counted 1 2 3 4 1 2 3 4 it's better to tap on 1 and 3 only. Then you can to tap fast rhythms too.

| 1 | + | 2 | + | 3 | + | 4 | + |
|---|---|---|---|---|---|---|---|
| TAP | | | | TAP | | | |

# 3 NEW GUITAR RHYTHMS

Strum Down
*Sound The Strings*

Strum Down
*Miss The Strings*

Strum Up
*Sound The Strings*

Strum Up
*Miss The Strings*

Strum Louder

The quickest way to master guitar rhythms is to mute the strings with your chord hand

**By Lightly Touching Them.**

Now you don't have the pressure of trying to play a song at the same time.

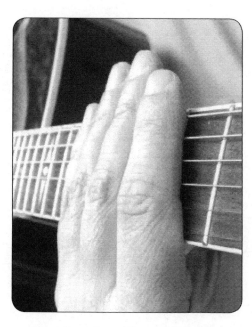

Dont Press Them Down

## RHYTHM 1

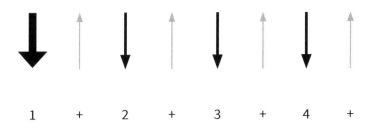

1     +     2     +     3     +     4     +

## RHYTHM 2

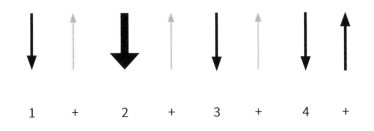

1     +     2     +     3     +     4     +

## RHYTHM 3

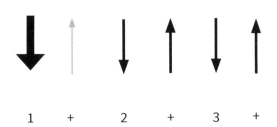

1     +     2     +     3     +

# PRACTICE PROGRAM

# LESSON 6

- Practice Finger Exercise - *Page 48*
- Practice Strumming - *Page 40*
- Practice Rolling - *Page 52*
- Practice 3 Rhythms - *Page 61*

---

# NOTES

# LESSON 7

4 NEW CHORDS

HOW TO CHANGE CHORDS FAST
STEP 1

HOW TO READ GUITAR TABLATURE

PERFECT HAND POSITIONING

# E M

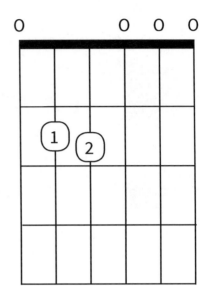

## STEP 1

## STEP 2

## STEP 3

Change from Em to E7sus4
*Without Moving* your 1st finger?

# E7 SUS4

## STEP 1

## STEP 2

## STEP 3

Change back to Em - *Without Moving* your 1st finger

When learning chords you improve much faster by working on two chords at a time. Why? Simply because you get to speed up the chord change also.

# Amaj7

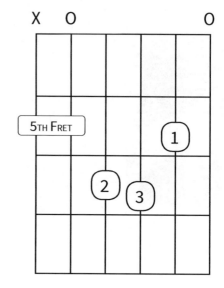

X     O           O

5th Fret

1

2

3

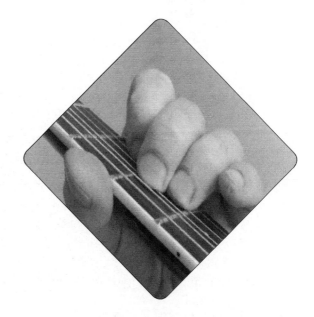

Thumb touching 6th string

# Bm SUS4

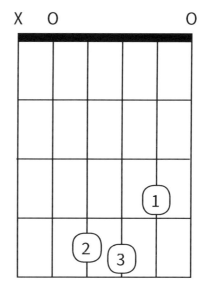

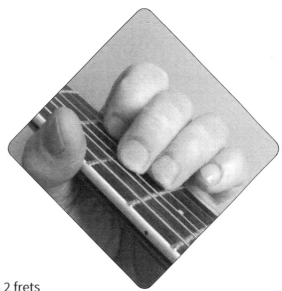

Keeping your fingers in the same
position as Amaj7, slide them down 2 frets

# HOW TO CHANGE CHORDS FAST

## STEP 1

When a finger is in the same position for a sequence of two or more chords you don't need to move it. It's called a pivot finger. Just keep it pressed down and pivot around it.

Most easy chord changes have a pivot finger. Difficult ones don't. There are many pivot finger chord changes on guitar. Here is an example.

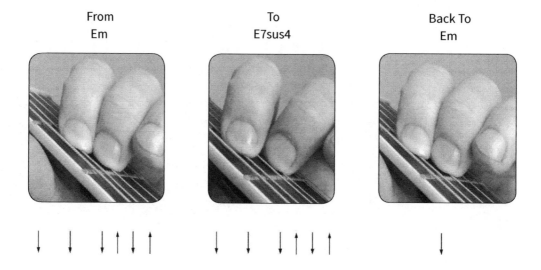

|         From          |          To           |       Back To       |
|         Em            |        E7sus4         |         Em          |

- Don't move 1st finger

- Maintain 1st fingertip pressure on string during the chord change

Learning guitar is much easier if you practice pivot finger changes first. Once you perfect them the feeling of continuity will soon transmit to more difficult changes.

From
A2

To
Dmaj9

Back To
A2

From
Em

To
A2

Back To
Em

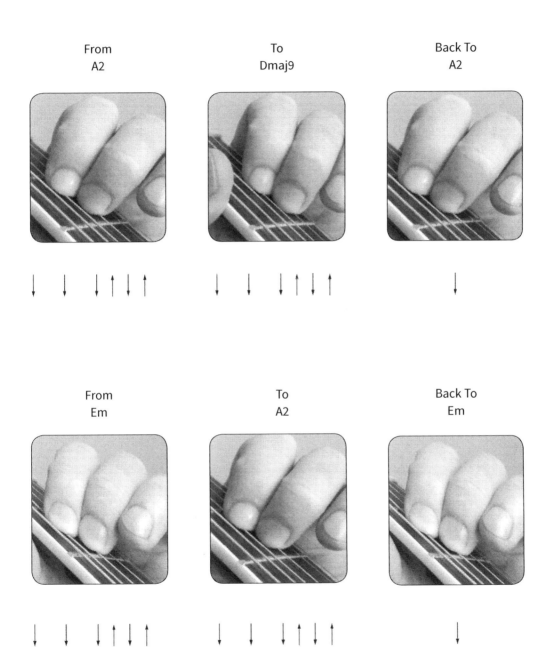

# HOW TO READ
# GUITAR TABLATURE

Guitar tablature is **Very Easy To Learn**. The six horizontal lines represent the six strings on the guitar. The top line is the 1st string and the bottom line is the 6th string. The numbers are the frets to play. 0 = Open String.  2 = 2nd Fret.

## EXAMPLE 1

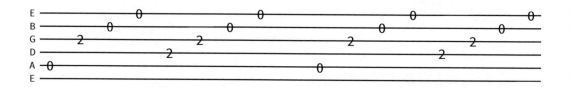

When numbers are one after another play each note one after another. You may notice that this tab plays the notes for A2 chord *(Page 20)*. Now finger A2 chord first and play the notes again.

## EXAMPLE 2

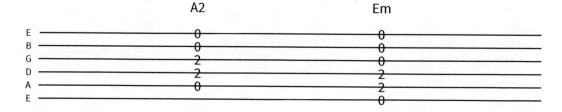

When numbers are on top of each other this indicates strumming. So all strings are played at the same time. Once you are familiar with chord shapes guitar tab will be even easier to follow.

# PERFECT HAND POSITIONING

Of all your fingers the 1st is the most important. Top guitarists place it in the corner at every opportunity. This makes chord changing much easier. It also pushes the other three fingers into the best playing position.

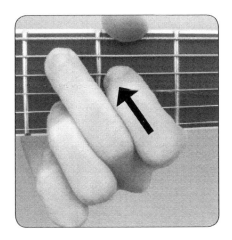

For chords such as A below, it's not possible. Instead you have to press the 1st fingertip harder for a clear sound.

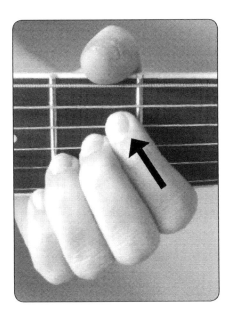

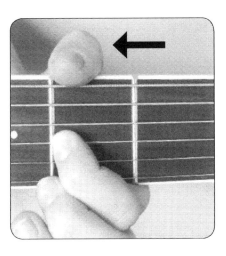

Slide your hand and thumb as one unit to push the 1st finger to the corner of a fret.

# PRACTICE PROGRAM

# LESSON 7

- Reread How Not To Play Guitar - *Page 10*

- Practice Finger Exercise - *Page 48*

- Practice 3 Rhythms - *Page 61*

- Practice New Chords - *Page 68 - 71*

- Practice Fast Chord Changing - *Page 72 - 73*

- Review Reading Guitar Tablature - *Page 74*

---

# NOTES

# LESSON 8

FINGERSTYLE GUITAR

LEAD GUITAR

HOW TO SKIP STRINGS

IMPROVERS FINGER EXERCISE

# FINGERSTYLE GUITAR

The hand set up for fingerstyle guitar is very similar to lead guitar. The heel pad of your hand can rest lightly on the bridge pins...and / or your 4th finger can lightly rest on the guitar.

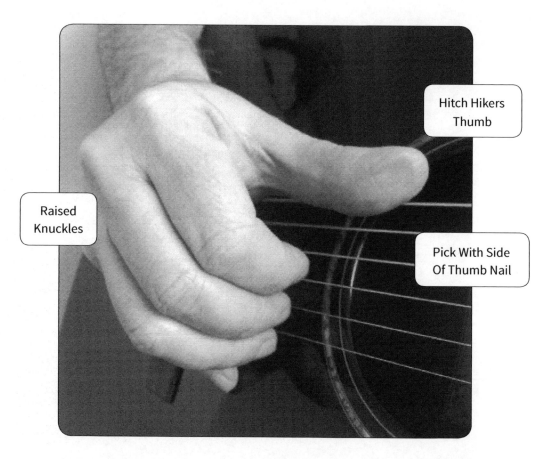

Hitch Hikers Thumb

Raised Knuckles

Pick With Side Of Thumb Nail

When picking strings your hand can slide up and down the bridge a little.

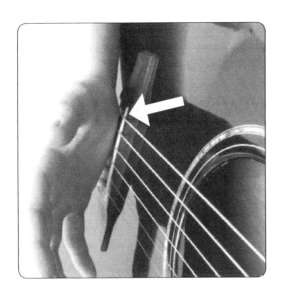

Competent guitarists play by feel and without looking at their picking hand. They do this by playing from a reference point.

Many have the heel pad of their hand lightly resting on the bridge pins (pictured left).

Others have the 4th finger on the guitar (below). Or maybe their 3rd and 4th fingers lightly touching it. You can also play with a combination of the two positions.

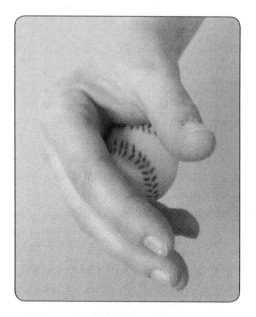

Visualize A Ball
In Your Hand

Top guitarists play with their knuckles level or above the fingertips.

Why? Because they power their fingers from the knuckles which gives a shorter but louder finger action. Its much easier to control.

Also it lets your fingernails approach the strings from straight on a bit like scoring from straight in front of goal.

If you dont set your knuckles high your fingers are left to pick the strings from underneath which is like trying to score from the sideline.

Its much harder and a very common fault among beginners.

Pick In
Circular Motion

Amaj7 - *Page 70*

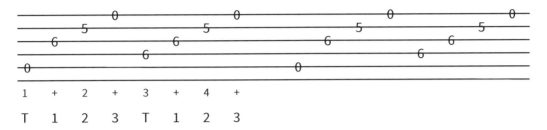

| 1 | + | 2 | + | 3 | + | 4 | + |
|---|---|---|---|---|---|---|---|
| T | 1 | 2 | 3 | T | 1 | 2 | 3 |

Bm sus4 - *Page 71*

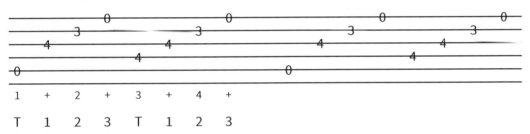

| 1 | + | 2 | + | 3 | + | 4 | + |
|---|---|---|---|---|---|---|---|
| T | 1 | 2 | 3 | T | 1 | 2 | 3 |

## PLAYING TIPS

Thumb picks *Down*

Thumb picks *A Little Louder* than fingers

Fingers pick *Up* at about a 60° angle

# LEAD GUITAR

The heel pad of your hand rests lightly on the bridge.

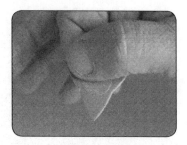

Rhythm Guitar
*Half*

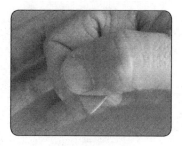

Lead Guitar
*Quarter*

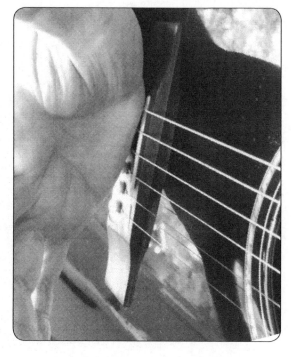

Hand can slide up and down the
bridge but not away from it

Here the 4th finger rests lightly on the guitar. It may slide up and down a little but always keeps contact and can be used as an alternative to the heel pad on the bridge.

*All Great Guitarists Play With Feel*. But to do so they need reference points like these. It's similar to typing which depends on good thumb positioning.

# HOW TO
# SKIP STRINGS

Here is *One Of The Great Secrets* of playing guitar - *Measured Picking*. Many people pick a string and then look for the next string in two seperate moves. This causes *A BLOCK* which makes it impossible to play fast on time.

A good picking action is usually

1   Picked in the direction of the next string

2   Measured exactly to the next string in one motion

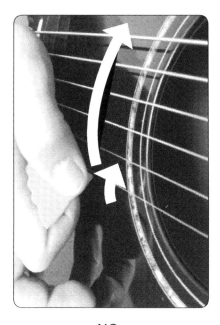

NO                          YES

Beginners tend to look at their rhythm   hand until they make a mistake with the other hand. Then they look at that hand.

But by the time they correct it the rhythm hand has gone wrong. Here's the cure.

A professional might quickly glance at both hands at the start of a song or lead line but thats only to position them. From there they may look at their chord hand but seldom if ever look at the other hand.

# IMPROVERS
# FINGER EXERCISE

This is a more difficult version of the finger exercise on *Page 48*. Now you're going to play it with both hands. You will also be practicing *18 Different Skills* at the same time. They are in all songs played on guitar.

1    Put the heel pad of your hand on the bridge of the guitar

2    Use about a *Quarter Of The Guitar Pick*

3    Position your *Thumb Low And Centred* behind the 2nd fret

4    Place all of your fingers on the 1st string, *One In Each Fret*

5    Press strings hard with your *Fingertips*

6    Start by moving your 1st Fingertip to the 5th string 1st fret. Pick the 5th string once and try for a clear sound.

7    Then move your 2nd fingertip to the 5th string 2nd fret. Pick once

8    Now move the 3rd fingertip to the 5th string 3rd Fret. Pick once

9    Then your 4th fingertip to the 5th string 4th fret. Pick once

Do the same on the next string. *The Complete Exercise* is on the next page.

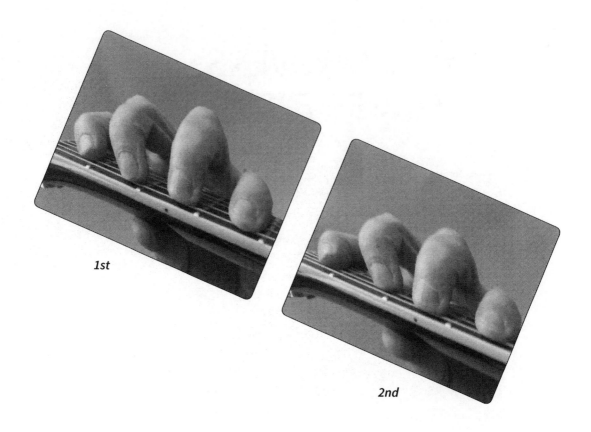

*1st*

*2nd*

Once you arrive at the finish you can practice back up one finger at a time.

Start with the 1st finger up one string, then the 2nd finger up one string, then the 3rd and so on until all four fingers are back on the sixth string.

You will find it much easier going back up.

# DID YOUR HAND CRAMP?

If it did, don't worry. It is quite normal. Rest it until you feel ready to start again. Once your hand is strong, it won't cramp anymore.

And you will find bar chords much easier to play too.

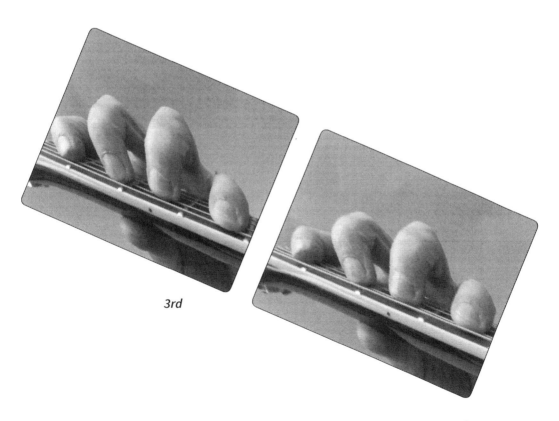

*3rd*

*4th*

# WEAK 3RD FINGER?

Most beginners find it difficult to learn chords simply because their *3rd Finger Is Weaker* than the others. Do you find it difficult to move your 3rd finger to the string you want? If so this exercise will help you greatly.

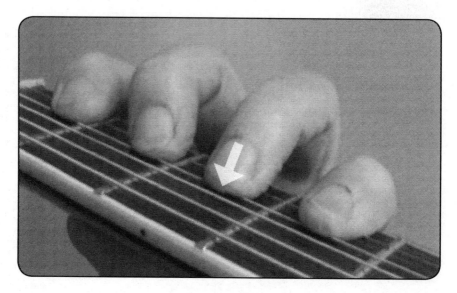

START HERE

Place all four fingertips on the 3rd string. Then start by moving the *3rd Fingertip Only* up one string. Then move it up another string as pictured on these pages.

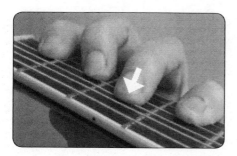

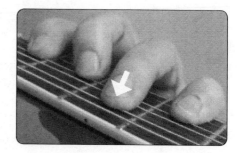

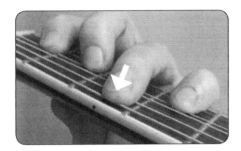 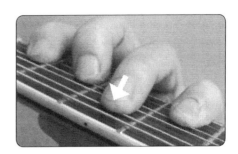

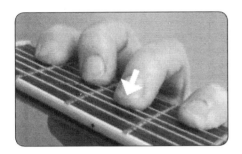 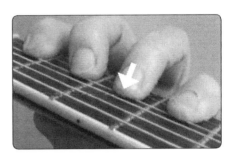

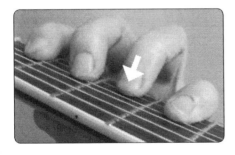 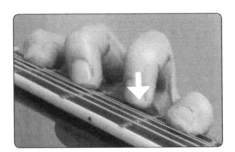

Did you see how difficult it was to come down to the 2nd and 1st strings? If you keep trying this, in just a few days it should be much easier.

Can you try the same exercise, but with your 4th finger this time? Again start on the 3rd string. You may find that it too needs to be strengthened. If so exercising your 4th finger will help you even more.

# PRACTICE PROGRAM

# LESSON 8

- Practice 3 Rhythms - *Page 61*
- Practice Fast Chord Changing - *Page 71 - 72*
- Practice Fingerstyle Hand Set-Up - *Page 78*
- Practice Measured Picking - *Page 83*
- Practice Finger Exercise - *Page 86*

---

# NOTES

# LESSON 9

3 NEW CHORDS

HOW TO CHANGE CHORDS FAST - STEP 2

THE BEST WAY TO PLAY OPEN CHORDS

THE HALF TRIANGLE

# CADD9

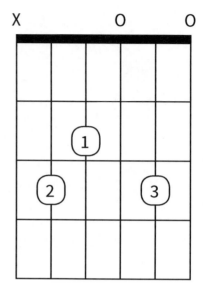

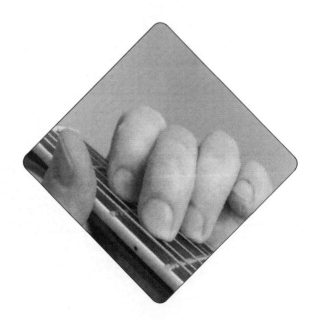

Can you change from Cadd9 to D - *Without Moving* your thumb or 3rd finger?

Can you change from D to Cadd9 - *Without Moving* your thumb or 3rd finger?

# D

X    O    O

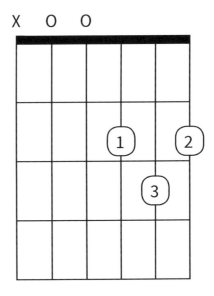

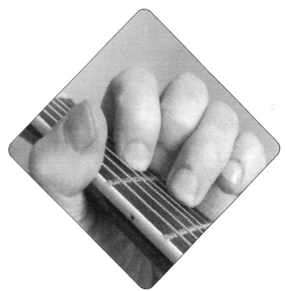

As you saw on *Page 69* it dramatically increases your speed of progress when you learn at least two chords at a time.

The real art of your chord hand is not only the chords you play. It's also what happens between them.

# G   ANOTHER WAY

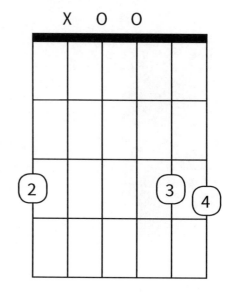

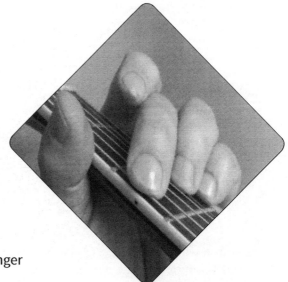

Thumb Not Touching 6th String

5th String *Muted* by Inside of 2nd Finger

# THE BEST WAY TO PLAY OPEN CHORDS

To play most open chords on natural ability your *Fingers Are Set Horizontal* to the frets.

Practice this with great care. It should soon become easy and effortless.

You can also set your hand by pretending to hold a rose. Then seperate your thumb and first finger the width of a guitar neck.

# HOW TO CHANGE CHORDS FAST
## *STEP 2*

### DON'T MOVE

- *Your Thumb*
- *3rd Finger*
- *Or Triangle*

This simple lesson keeps your fingers close to the fretboard. Because they have less distance to travel back to the strings when needed, your chord changing becomes much faster.

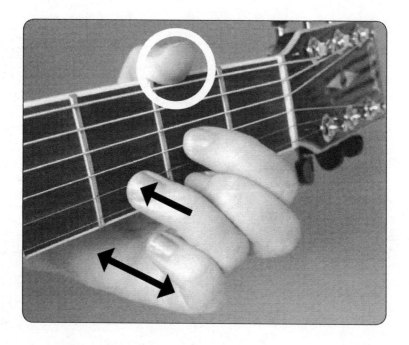

You can play *Tens of Thousands of Songs* on guitar without moving your thumb, 3rd finger, or triangle.

If you look closely at all these chords you'll see that

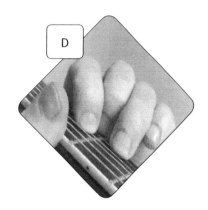

D

1   The 3rd finger is in the same place for all of them

2   The 3rd finger stays *Constantly Pressed* into the string even during chord changes

3   The Guitar Triangle

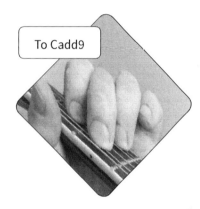

To Cadd9

The 1st and 2nd fingers do most of the changing. Your hand stays almost still.

This position combined with keeping your 3rd finger pressed down also keeps the fingertips close to the fretboard.

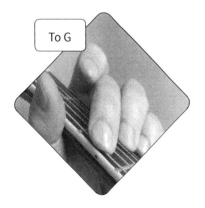

To G

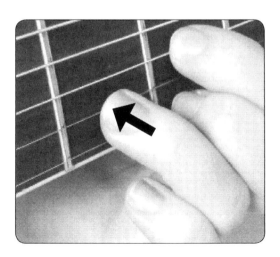

3rd finger stays pressed down
during these chord changes

## SONG EXAMPLE

## *FREE FALLING*

Capo
3RD FRET

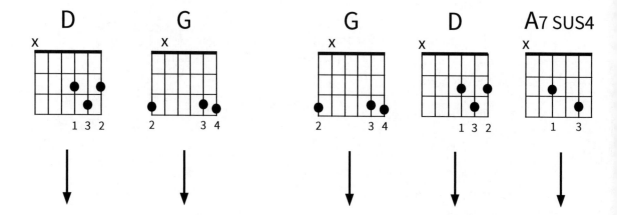

D    G    G    D    A7 SUS4

## PLAYING TIPS

Keep repeating this chord sequence

*Dont Move* - Your thumb 3rd finger, or triangle (*Page 96*)

**FULL SONG** → GUITAR-PRO.COM

# THE HALF TRIANGLE

"The Guitar Triangle" is one of the secrets of playing guitar. It creates space for your fingers to move.

This makes chord changing much *Quicker - Easier and More Natural*. For chords like B7 and E you'll need about a "Half Triangle".

Thumb Stays
On Top

Go From
*Full* Triangle
To *Half* Triangle

When changing back to D it's vital that you reopen the full triangle. If you don't your fingers will have nowhere to go.

Now you're ready to start learning your favourite songs while continuing here. And any books or lessons that confused you before, will make much more sense now.

# BE CAREFUL

However, avoid F, B, and barre chords. It's still too soon to learn these.

## PRACTICE PROGRAM

## LESSON 9

- Practice Finger Exercise - *Page 86*
- Practice D, Cadd9, G - *Page 97*
- Practice Fast Chord Changing - *Page 72 - 73*
- Practice 3 Rhythms - *Page 61*
- Reread How Not To Play Guitar - *Page 10*

# LESSON 10

### YOUR FAVOURITE SONGS
### IN 3 STEPS

### 4 NEW CHORDS

### HOW TO CHANGE CHORDS FAST
### STEP 3

### NEW GUITAR RHYTHM

# YOUR FAVOURITE SONGS

## *IN 3 STEPS*

The quickest way to find chords for a song is on Google. But you will have two problems. First of all, G chord is often not shown to you as played by professional guitarists. And secondly, you're not given strum patterns for most songs.

This Simple 3 Step Guide

- Is the solution to both problems
- Should enable you to learn your favourite songs
- Saves you a huge amount of time

For best results start with very slow songs . As you improve you can play faster songs.

# STEP 1

### *SONG EXAMPLE*

## Happy Birthday To You

 Happy birthday to you guitar chords

Note: beginners can play the **chord** of D instead of $D^7$, as the notes in the two **chords** are almost the same (actually, **you** can do this in many songs). **Guitar chords**: These are the **chord** charts for **Happy Birthday** in key G, suitable for playing on acoustic or electric **guitar**.

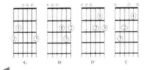

Happy Birthday chords with lyrics and guitar chord chart sheet
recordrestorations.com/chords-happy-birthday.php

*About this result • Feedback*

HAPPY BIRTHDAY CHORDS by Misc Traditional @ Ultimate-Guitar ...
https://tabs.ultimate-guitar.com/m/misc_traditional/happy_birthday_crd.htm ▾
★★★★✦ Rating: 4.7 - 863 reviews
Apr 15, 2009 - [Intro] / A D / D A Happy Birthday to You D Happy Birthday to You G Happy Birthday
dear "fill in name here" D A D Happy Birthday to You / Hey ...

*Avoid This G - (Page 104)*

```
            G           D
Happy  birthday  to  you


            D           G
Happy  birthday  to  you


            G             C
Happy  birthday  dear  _____


            G         D G
Happy  birthday  to  you
```

# STEP 2

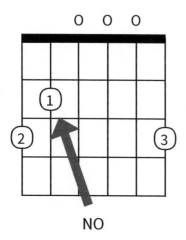

NO

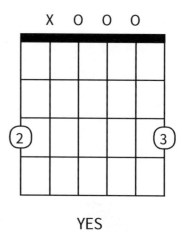

YES

Often G chord is not shown to you correctly. Professional guitarists mute the 5th string with the inside of the finger playing the 6th string.

YES

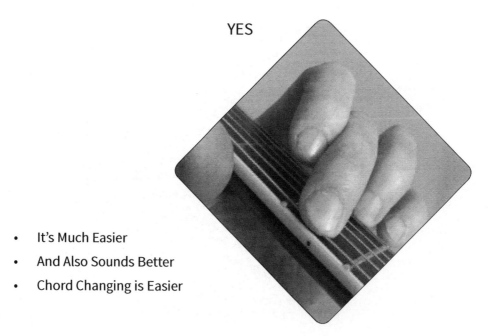

- It's Much Easier
- And Also Sounds Better
- Chord Changing is Easier

# STEP 3

The easiest way to learn a good strum pattern is to find a good guitar lesson for the same song on YouTube. Once you find one you that's easy to follow you may still have the G problem. Again, play G as in Step 2.

 Happy birthday to you guitar lesson

Happy Birthday To You - Acoustic Guitar Lesson - (easy)

Alan Robinson

3 years ago • 853,342 views

An acoustic guitar lesson of my interpretation of the traditional song - Happy Birthday to You, inspired by my dog, Molly's 10th ...

Happy Birthday EASY Guitar Tutorial (How to play)

Andy Guitar

1 year ago • 729,463 views

SUBSCRIBE ►► http://goo.gl/nDtSmJ Happy Birthday TAB FREE ...

How To Play Happy Birthday on Guitar

Guitarjamz

6 years ago • 2,458,105 views

Free Ebook when you sign my email list !! http://www.guitarjamz.com/new_requests/ Links : Site...

You will find G C and D chords in many songs you want to learn. Try replacing them with G Cadd9 D *(Page 97)*. Continue to play the song this way if it's

- Easier To Play
- Sounds Better
- Chord Changing Is Easier

# Cmaj7

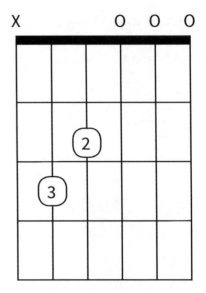

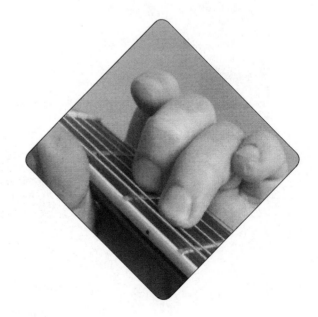

Thumb Touching 6th String

# D/E

X    X    O        O

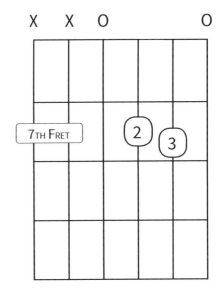

7TH FRET   ② ③

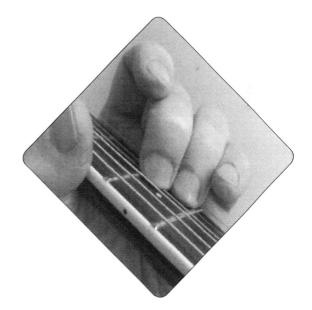

Thumb Can Touch 6th String

Strum 4 Strings

# Am

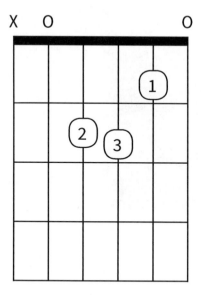

Thumb Touching 6th String

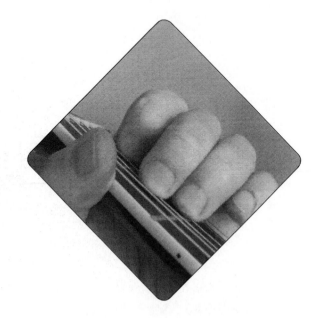

# E

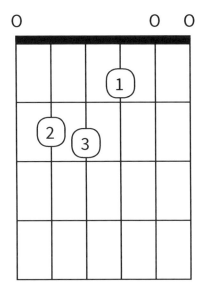

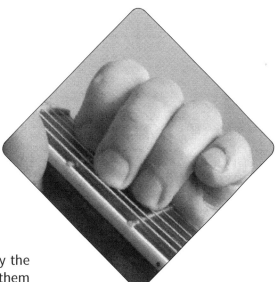

For E your fingers remain in exactly the same position as Am and you move them up one string.

# HOW TO CHANGE CHORDS FAST

## *STEP 3*

Here is an invaluable learning technique. Most beginners get into great difficulty when they try to change fast from one chord to another. Here, we are going to divide this very difficult step, into two easier ones.

| Am | To | E |
|---|---|---|

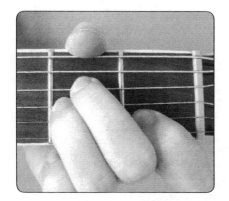 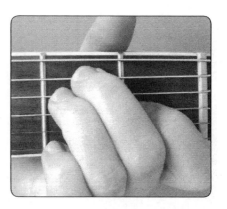

Raise Your Thumb

# STEP 1

## S L O W L Y

Move 3 Fingers
Up 1 String
- *As 1 Unit* -

# STEP 2

## VERY QUICKLY

Move 3 Fingers
Up 1 String
- *As 1 Unit* -

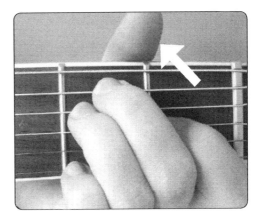

Raise Your Thumb

## VERY QUICKLY

Move 3 Fingers
Down 1 String
- *As 1 Unit* -

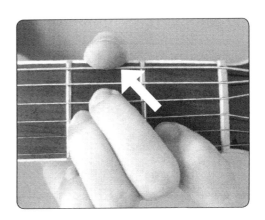

Thumb Touching 6th String

At this stage do not wait to check if your chord change is right or wrong.
Bounce from chord to chord without delay and immediately back again.

Here is another of the secrets of playing guitar. Whether you are an international star, or only playing a few weeks, you play D, C, or any chord the same way. D is D and C is C. However, what happens between the chords is the big difference.

The greats make it look easy because there is no waste movement between the chords. This is done by keeping unused fingers in a chord...and all fingers during a chord change, close to the fretboard.

To change chords well, start moving your fingers in the direction of the new chord, during the last upstroke of your present chord.

If you don't do this you will have a muddy sound at the start of the next chord you play. Get it right and two things happen:

1   The Sound Is Much *Clearer*

2   The Chord Change Is *Easier*

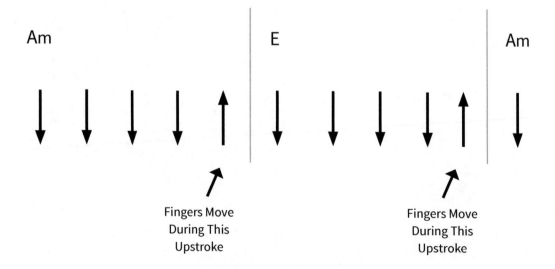

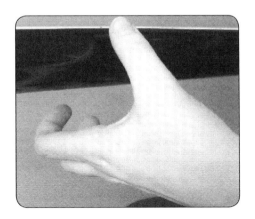

To lift something that requires strength your fingers naturally firm up. To finger chords your fingers need to firm up too.

Stretching your hand helps you to **Power Down The Strings** to get good sound.

It also keeps your fingers close to the fretboard during chord changes.

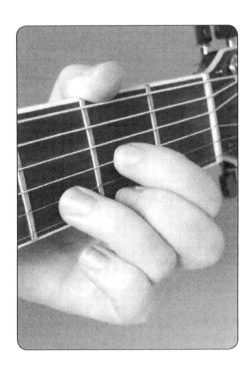

# NEW
# GUITAR RHYTHM

Rhythm 3 *(Page 65)* can be clearly heard in many famous songs. However, counting  1  2  3  1  2  3  1  2  3  1  2  3  can be very repetitive and boring. The rhythm becomes much more interesting if you count

| | | | |
|---|---|---|---|
| 1 | For The First | 1 2 3 | |
| 2 | For The Second | 1 2 3 | |
| 3 | For The Third | 1 2 3 | |
| 4 | For The Fourth | 1 2 3 | |

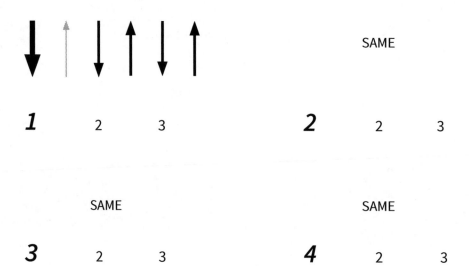

# PRACTICE PROGRAM

# LESSON 10

- Practice Improvers Finger Exercise - *Page 86*

- Practice Am and E - *Page 111*

- Practice Fast Chord Changing - *Page 97*

- Practice Fast Chord Changing - *Page 72 - 73*

- Practice New Guitar Rhythm - *Page 114*

---

# NOTES

Have you come this far Step by Step?

If so ... *You Have Done A Great Job!*

# CONGRATULATIONS

## Now You Can Play Guitar

Even if you have not fully mastered every lesson you're still doing very well. Any new discipline can be painful, but only for a short time.

*It Does Get Easier*. So the most important thing right now is to understand these lessons. In time they become a permanent part of your playing style.

You have enough guitar chords, rhythms and playing skills for a lifetime of enjoyment. Many people are quite happy with this. However if you want to continue, that's fine too.

But remember that these lessons are very carefully structured in order of difficulty. As in the beginners section, it is not a good idea to skip lessons. Or to move too fast from one lesson to the next.

There are two exception to this. "*Lesson 19*" will help you greatly too. As well as being able to change guitar strings, you'll know how to make your guitar easier to play, and sound better.

And "*Lesson 20*" contains most of the chords to your favourite songs. So you can reference them any time you're learning a new song.

Now back to the lessons again.

# LESSON 11

## 9
### POPULAR
### GUITAR RHYTHMS

## RHYTHM 1

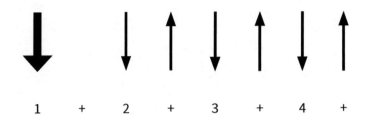

## RHYTHM 2

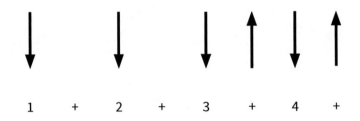

## RHYTHM 3

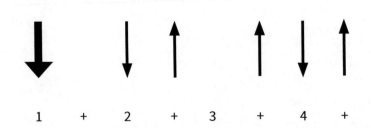

# RHYTHM 4

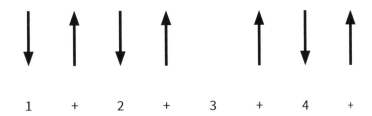

| 1 | + | 2 | + | 3 | + | 4 | + |

# RHYTHM 5

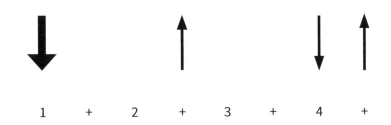

| 1 | + | 2 | + | 3 | + | 4 | + |

Professionals often combine two single rhythms
to avoid repetition. They might play

| Rhythm 2 | *First* | 4 Beats |
| Rhythm 5 | *Second* | 4 Beats |
| Rhythm 2 | *Third* | 4 Beats |
| Rhythm 5 | *Fourth* | 4 Beats |

Two more examples of this would be combining rhythms 3 and 6 or rhythms 8 and 2. Single rhythms are also sometimes combined with double rhythms.

You can mix and match any of them and make up your own. Again the quickest way to master them is to vamp the strings with your chord hand.

- Songs are also played in 3 beat rhythms

- They are often played fast

- You will need to practice them slowly at first

# RHYTHM 6

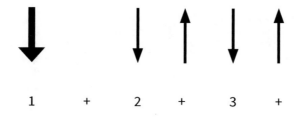

# RHYTHM 7

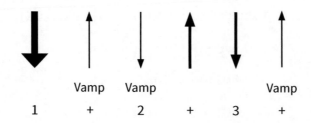

You can also mix and match single and double rhythms. Here are two of most used patterns. Because they're more difficult to perfect most people have to practice them S L O W at first.

## PLAYING TIP

Almost everybody's strumming gets loud when they start speeding up for the first time. But most rhythms are actually *Played Quite Softly, Even When Playing Fast*.

## RHYTHM 8

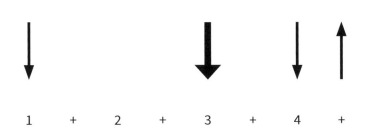

## RHYTHM 9

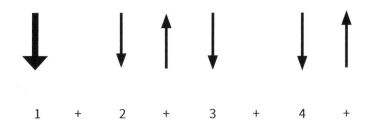

# PRACTICE PROGRAM

# LESSON 11

- Practice The 3 Rhythms - *Page 118*

- Practice Finger Exercise - *Page 86*

- Practice Am and E - *Page 111*

- Practice Fast Chord Changing - *Page 97*

- Practice New Guitar Rhythm - *Page 114*

---

# NOTES

# LESSON 12

HOW TO PLAY G - COMPLETE

2 NEW CHORDS

HOW TO CHANGE CHORDS FAST
STEP 4

# HOW TO PLAY G

## *COMPLETE*

As previously mentioned, learning G is one of the key reasons why people give up playing guitar. Learning it wrong can lead to many unnecessary obstacles later on.

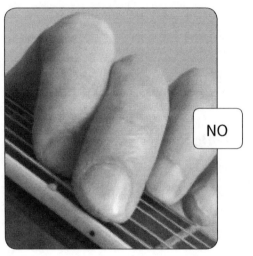

NO

- It never quite sounds right

- It makes changing to C and D quite difficult

- It limits your ability to add bass runs and ornamentation

YES

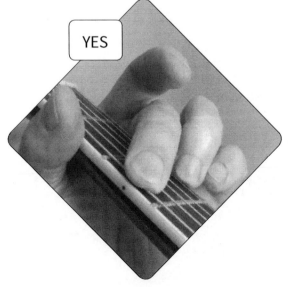

If you play G like this, lift your first finger to mute the 5th string.

It will sound much better and you can continue to play it until you have perfected the two more difficult G's on the next page.

As well as giving you more musical options, they make chord changing easier too. You strum 6 strings, but only 5 sound.

# WITH THIS G

YES

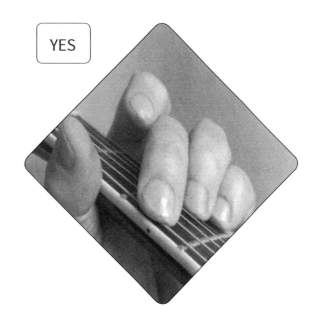

Em is mostly played with the 1st and 2nd fingers.

Also you won't have to move your 3rd finger when changing to D, Cadd9 or Em7.

You get a *Rich Sound.*

# WITH THIS G

YES

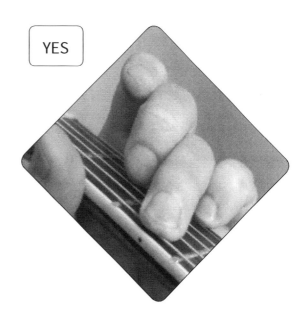

Em is mostly played with the 2nd and 3rd fingers.

2nd and 3rd fingers move as one unit when changing to C D and other chords.

It frees up your 1st and 2nd fingers to add bass runs, and ornamentation.

# G  3RD WAY

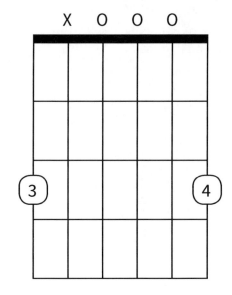

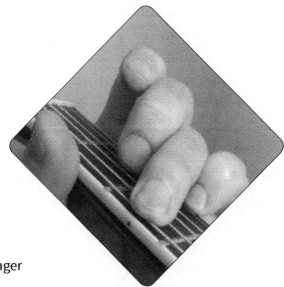

**5th String *Muted* By Inside of 3rd Finger**

If their hand is big enough, top guitarists keep the thumb touching the 6th string, even though it does not impact on sound.

It does however, save them moving it on the next chord change often, because it's already preset for that chord. You may not be able to do this if your hand is small.

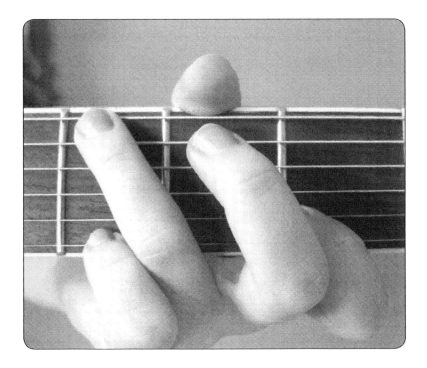

Learning G professionally is more difficult....but it does pay off. Top guitarists play it at least three different ways, which opens up

*A Lifetime of Endless Possibilities*.

# C

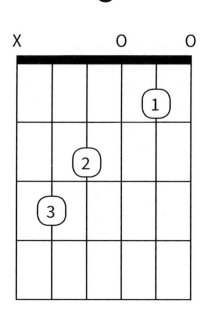

Thumb Touching 6th String

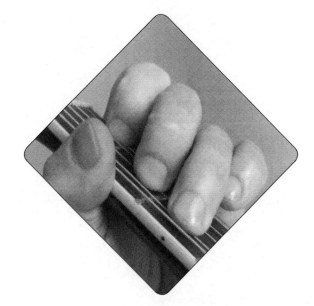

# FMAJ7

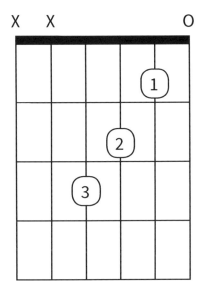

Thumb Touching 6th String

1st String Must Sound

# HOW TO CHANGE CHORDS FAST
## *STEP 4*

## THE MAGIC MOVE

Here is another great secret of playing guitar. It's in millions of songs. You need to be able to *Move Your 2nd and 3rd Fingers As One Unit*. Once perfected, it speeds up hundreds of chord changes up, down, and across the fretboard.

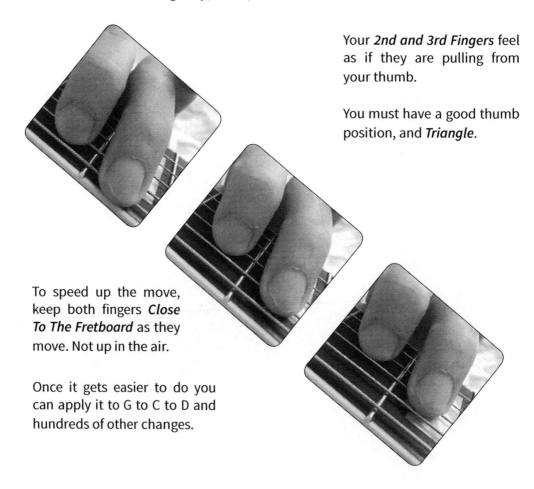

Your *2nd and 3rd Fingers* feel as if they are pulling from your thumb.

You must have a good thumb position, and *Triangle*.

To speed up the move, keep both fingers *Close To The Fretboard* as they move. Not up in the air.

Once it gets easier to do you can apply it to G to C to D and hundreds of other changes.

The Magic Move needs to be practiced very *S L O W L Y* for a few days. Then you can *Speed It Up.*

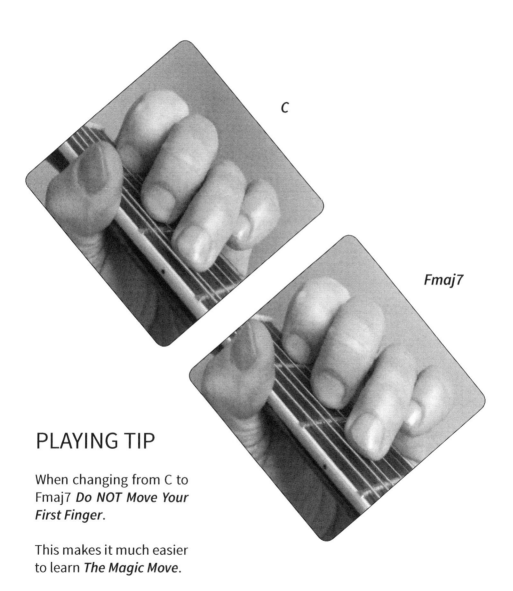

*C*

*Fmaj7*

## PLAYING TIP

When changing from C to Fmaj7 *Do NOT Move Your First Finger*.

This makes it much easier to learn *The Magic Move*.

# THE MAGIC MOVE
# MADE EASY

If you cannot change quick enough it can be very helpful to hold your rhythm hand in the up-position. Now it is ready for the next downstroke, as you practice changing chords.

- Start moving your 1st and 2nd fingers *As A Unit* during the last upstroke.

- Put them on just before the first downstroke of the next chord.

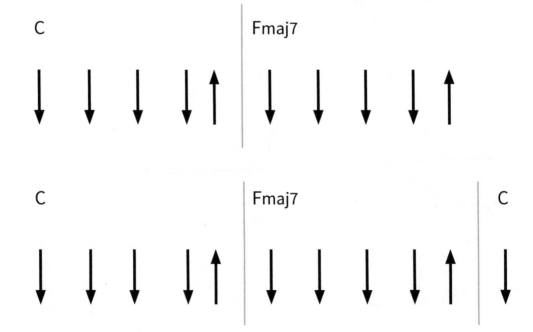

# YOUR FINGER NAILS

Your finger nails can be two different lengths. Chord hand nails must always be short. Otherwise it will be impossible to produce good sound. You can have them longer on your rhythm hand for fingerstyle guitar.

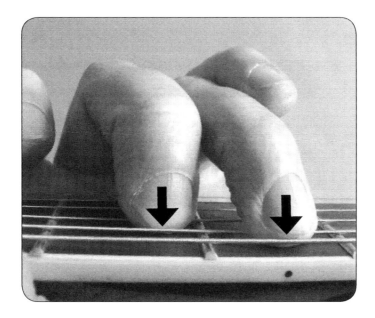

Your fingertips and nails can also be used to touch and mute strings such as the 5th and 6th on C as shown here. You push up to the string *Above* the finger to free the string *Below* it.

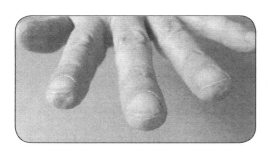

Chord Hand
*Short Nails*

# YOUR 4TH FINGER

Does your 4th finger jump up as you change from D to G? This is caused by not having The Triangle.

1    Finger D chord with *The Triangle*

2    *Hold 4th Finger* as shown here just before you change

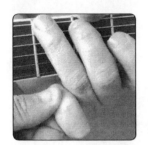

3    *Very Slowly* move 2nd and 3rd fingers up to G

4    Then *Push 4th Finger* onto the 1st string and let it go

5    Now move fingers back to D

6    As they come down make sure to *Reopen The Triangle*

7    *Hold 4th Finger* and start again

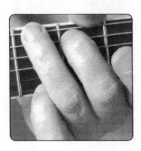

This learning technique is not easy and has to be practiced very slowly for a few days. Then you gradually speed it up. It helps greatly to overcome the problem.

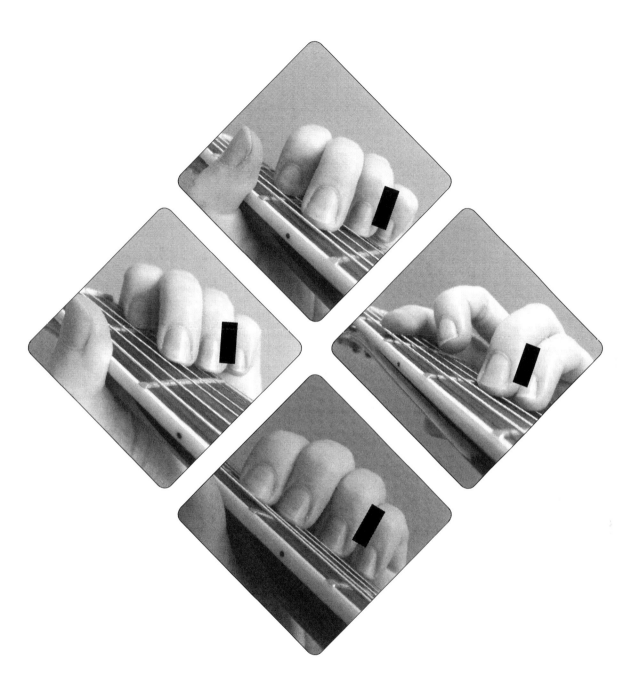

Pofessional guitarists often *Link Their 3rd and 4th fingers*. It makes them stronger. And it makes *Two Fingers Feel Like One* which is much easier to control.

# PRACTICE PROGRAM

# LESSON 12

- Practice G - *Page 124*

- Practice C - *Page 128*

- Practice The Magic Move *VERY SLOWLY* - *Page 130*

- Practice Changing From C to Fmaj7 - *Page 131*

- Practice 4th Finger Exercise - *Page 134*

---

# NOTES

# LESSON 13

WHAT IS A CAPO FOR?

HOW TO PLAY F

# WHAT IS A CAPO FOR?

You now have the top 50 chords in all music styles on your guitar *(Page 197)*. Simply by buying a a capo you increase that to 500 chords. A capo can be placed on up to ten frets. Even though you play with the same chord positions, you get a different set of sounds for each fret that the capo is on.

Also the guitar should be pitched to the vocalist in order to retain the quality of their voice. If the singer comes back to the instrument they lose their vocal quality - and then their audience.

The words of our favourite songs mean much to us and all good guitarists play in the key that best suits the voice. Its often done with a capo.

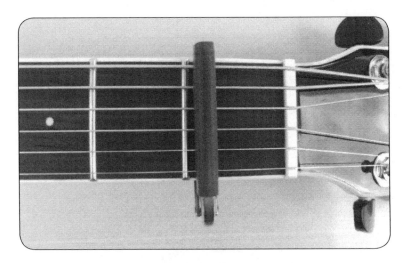

Capo 1st Fret

If a song suits your voice that's great. If it doesn't try putting a capo on the 1st fret. It has now replaced the nut on your guitar which means that what was the 2nd fret has now become the new 1st fret.

All you have to do is play the same chord sequence again and the song is in a higher key. If this position suits your voice that's great. If not you can move it up or down as many frets as you like until it suits.

# 3 TYPES OF CAPO

**Curved**    Suits most acoustic
              and electric guitars

**Straight**  Suits nylon string
              classical guitars

**12
String**      Suits 12 string and
              wide necked guitars

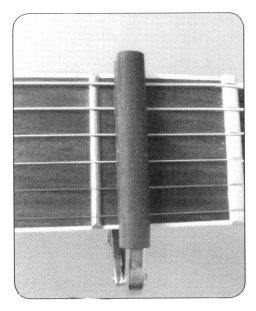

You should always place the capo as close as possible to the steel fret, within a 1/4 inch from the fret.

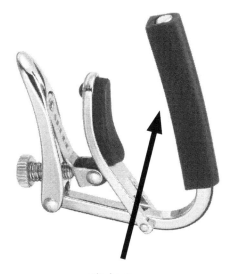

Slight Curve

Before buying a capo check to see if the fretboard of your guitar is *Straight Or Curved*. Then you will know which one you need.

If you find it hard to get a good sound put a capo on the 1st fret. Now it is easier to press the strings.

Once you've got the sound take off your capo.

# HOW TO PLAY F

## WHY IS F SO DIFFICULT?

All chords are played from either the Thumb / Triangle hand position or The Bar Chord hand position. *F Is The Exception.* It does *NOT* have a triangle. And it's played with a different thumb position.

## TRY THIS

*GRAB* the guitar neck first

Then move your fingers into position

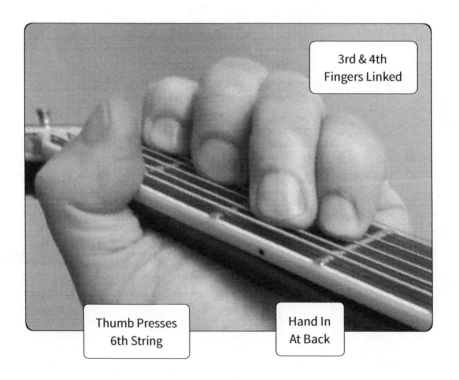

3rd & 4th Fingers Linked

Thumb Presses 6th String

Hand In At Back

Many people spend a lifetime struggling with F. Because it is usually the first chord they need where two strings are pressed by the same finger. Many of them pull the hand out from behind the guitar neck.

*THIS IS FATAL*.

The palm of your hand must go *In And Up* behind the guitar.

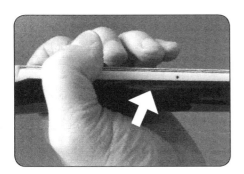 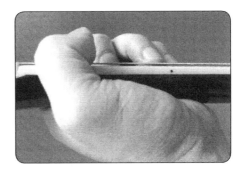

*Look Behind The Guitar Neck.* Try grabbing the guitar at the top, with your thumb over the 6th string.

At the same time, move your fingers into the F chord position, with the *Thumb Rolling Sideways.* It should press the 6th string 1st fret for a deeper sound.

If you can retain a good sound while holding the guitar in one hand you can play F really well.

# F

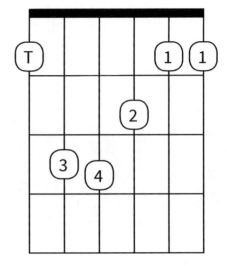

Grab The
Guitar Neck

Thumb *Pressing* 6th String 1st Fret

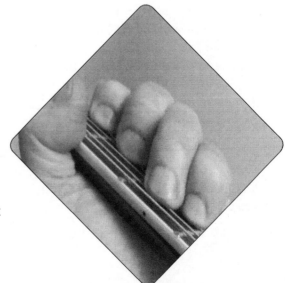

# Dm7

X    X    O

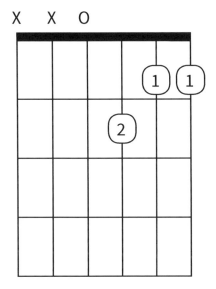

Grab The
Guitar Neck

Thumb Touching 6th String

# PRACTICE PROGRAM

# LESSON 13

- Practice Finger Exercise - *Page 86*

- Pracitce The Magic Move *FASTER* - *Page 130*

- Practice Changing From G to C to D with The Magic Move

- Practice Changing From C to Fmaj7 - *Page 131*

- Practice 4th Finger Exercise - *Page 134*

---

# NOTES

# LESSON 14

## HOW TO PLAY
## BARRE CHORDS

## HOW TO MAKE
## BARRE CHORDS EASIER

## HOW TO CHANGE TO
## BARRE CHORDS

# HOW TO PLAY
# BARRE CHORDS

The word barre can be very misleading. Most people interpret it literally and bar their first finger straight. If you look at any top guitarist, you will clearly see that

### *The First Finger Is Curved And Turned Out*.

1   Copy the curved finger below

2   Nail turned out about 30°

3   This is the same as barring on a guitar

4   For most power chords the first finger presses only one string - *The 6th or 5th*

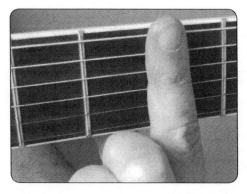

NO

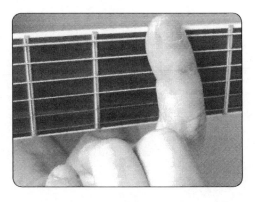

YES

You also need a good thumb and wrist position. It has to be low and fairly centred. Your wrist should be low too.

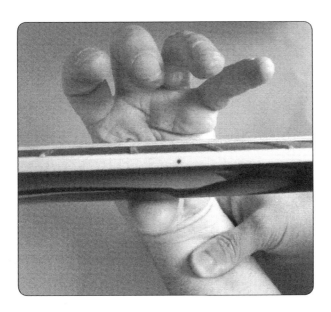

This is not as easy to do as it looks. If you're having difficulty it will help to ask a friend to hold your wrist in position as shown here.

After a few minutes, you should start finding it easier to do.

Turning your bar finger out about a 30° angle helps greatly to bring the other fingers out in front of the fretboard and in line with the strings.

Now barre and power chords should be easier to play.

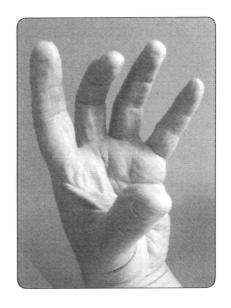

# HOW TO MAKE BARRE CHORDS EASIER

To play barre and power chords on natural ability your *Fingers Are Set Parallell* to the frets. Practice this with great care. It should soon become easy and effortless.

- Fingers *NARROW* as you slide towards bridge

- Fingers *WIDEN* as you slide towards tuning heads

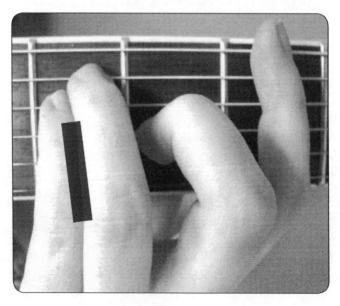

For barre chords your 3rd and
4th fingers should be linked together

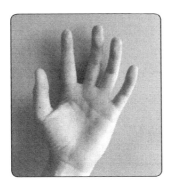

To make barre chords easier can you *Stretch* your hand and *Link* the 3rd and 4th fingers?

Your hand now feels as if it has only three fingers. This is easier to control, especially when you're changing chords.

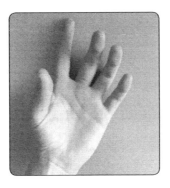

Playing guitar is much easier when you make

4 Feel Like 3

3 Feel Like 2

2 Feel Like 1

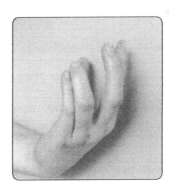

It's done by always looking for opportunities to link your fingers. You can even practice barre chord and power chord shapes without a guitar *If You Stretch Your Hand First*.

# HOW TO CHANGE TO BARRE CHORDS

Finger C chord with your *Thumb On Top*. Slide your *Thumb Only* down at the back. Keeping it centred, slowly *Tilt The Guitar Neck By Leaning Forward*. Your fingers should be still in the C position.

With your hand *Stretched* move fingers into the Bm chord while in the air.

Now drop Bm chord onto the fretboard.

Many top guitarists start sliding the thumb down behind the neck from the second beat of the open chord they are playing. It is fully in position for the barre or power chord before the fourth beat is played.

# 5 SKILLS
# TOP GUITARISTS SHARE

1  Thumb *Low* and *Centred*

2  1st finger *Curved*

3  Thumb and fingers *Stretched*

4  3rd and 4th fingers *Linked*

5  Fingers *Narrow and Widen* as you move up and down the fretboard

Professionals can do all these skills at the same time. And if you practice them individually, you will soon find barre and power chords much easier to play.

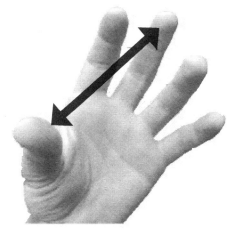

Pushing your thumb against the 1st finger helps greatly to improve sound.

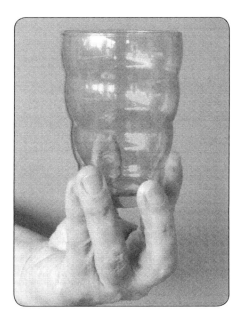

Your hand should feel as if you are holding a glass full of water. Then link your 3rd and 4th fingers.

If you like, try holding the glass, linking your 3rd and 4th fingers together.

Then remove the glass and you are left with a perfect hand for barre and power chords. Hold this hand shape as you approach the guitar neck from underneath.

# PRACTICE PROGRAM

# LESSON 14

- Practice Finger Exercise - *Page 86*

- Practice 1st Finger Position - *Page 146*

- Practice Hand Position With Glass - *Page 149*

- Pracitce The Magic Move *FASTER* - *Page 130*

---

# NOTES

.

# LESSON 15

E

SHAPED

BARRE CHORDS

# E SHAPED
# BARRE CHORDS

## STEP 1

Learn these notes on the *6th String*

| FRET | NOTE |
|:---:|:---:|
| O | E |
| 1st | F |
| 3rd | G |
| 5th | A |
| 7th | B |
| 8th | C |
| 10th | D |
| 12th | E |

Your Hand Must Approach
From Underneath

# STEP 2

E

Now we know all the notes on the 6th string, we can play an E chord.

Now remove your 1st finger, and play the E chord again with your 2nd 3rd and 4th fingers instead.

You may find that you have to press down slightly harder.

# STEP 3

Now lower your thumb and at the very same time, add your 1st finger across and outside the nut.

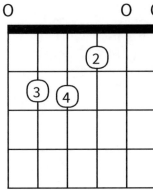

Lift your 2nd finger as shown here and you have Em.

If you also strum the 6th, 5th and 4th strings together you have E5, which is also known as E power chord.

From Em - Can you move your 4th finger down one string? This is E7sus4.

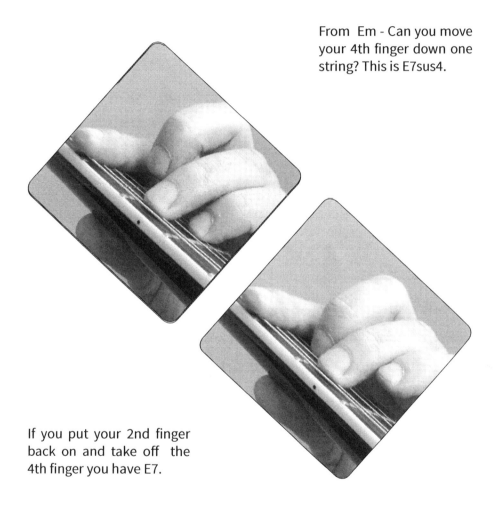

If you put your 2nd finger back on and take off the 4th finger you have E7.

If you move up one fret and repeat the chord sequence you get F, F7sus4 and Fm. The note your first finger presses on the 6th string is F. This helps to give you the name of the chords.

This combined with the finger changes, make it a 7 or sus4 or 7 and many more. The 3rd fret would give you all the G bar chord shapes because your 1st finger is playing G note on the 6th string. The 4th fret gives you the G# bar chords.

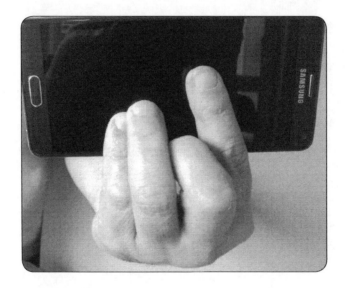

Practice on your phone
or The Mini Guitar

If you're having difficulty, with any of these moves, it's highly likely that your thumb has moved out of position behind the neck. To succeed with barre and power chords

***You Must Maintain A Good Thumb Position.***

# F#

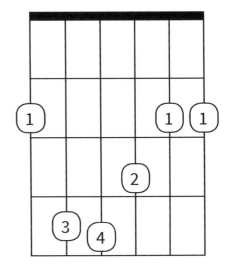

This is the barre chord
played on the 2nd fret

# F#M

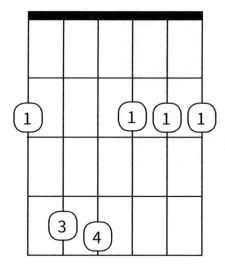

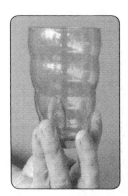

To play an F#m, simply remove
your 2nd finger from F#

# Gb

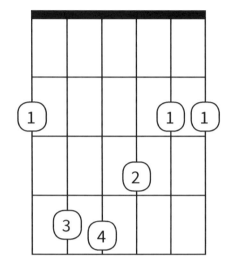

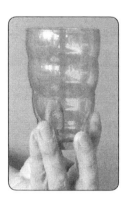

The F# barre chord is
also known as a Gb

# B

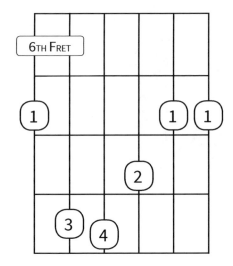

6TH FRET

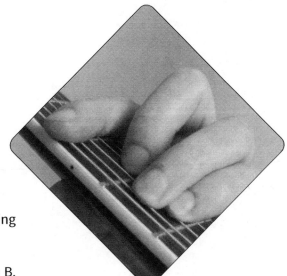

To play a B, simply slide everything up to the 7th fret.

The 6th string 7th fret is the note B. And with an E chord shape, that gives you the B barre chord.

# PRACTICE PROGRAM

# LESSON 15

- Practice Finger Exercise - *Page 86*

- Practice Step 1 - *Page 154*

- Practice Step 2 - *Page 155*

- Practice Step 3 - *Page 156*

---

# NOTES

# LESSON 16

## A

### SHAPED

### BARRE CHORDS

# A SHAPED
# BARRE CHORDS

Top guitarists also play A shaped barre chords. With E shaped barre chords only, you'll be constantly going up and down the guitar neck. However, by combining E and A shapes, many chord sequences can be played between three frets.

If you have followed the 3 steps to learning the E shaped chords, all you have to do is follow the same approach here. This now gives you over 200 chords to choose from.

## STEP 1

Learn these notes on the *5th String*

| FRET | NOTE |
|:---:|:---:|
| O | A |
| 2nd | B |
| 3rd | C |
| 5th | D |
| 7th | E |
| 8th | F |
| 10th | G |
| 12th | A |

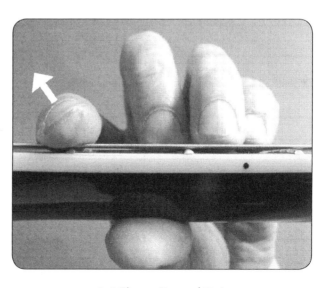

1st Finger Turned Out

# STEP 2

## AM

X    O          O

Try fingering an Am chord

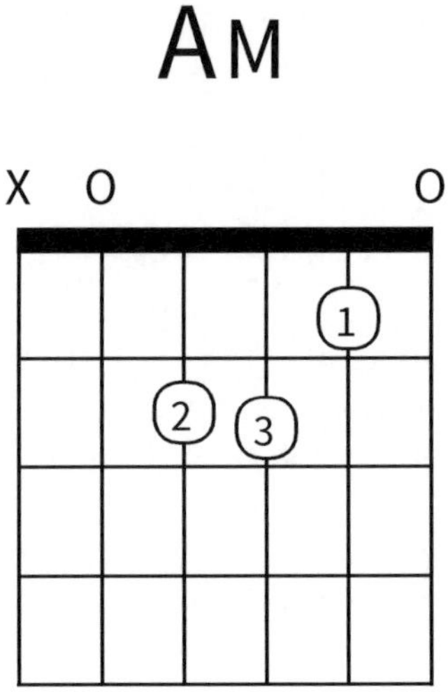

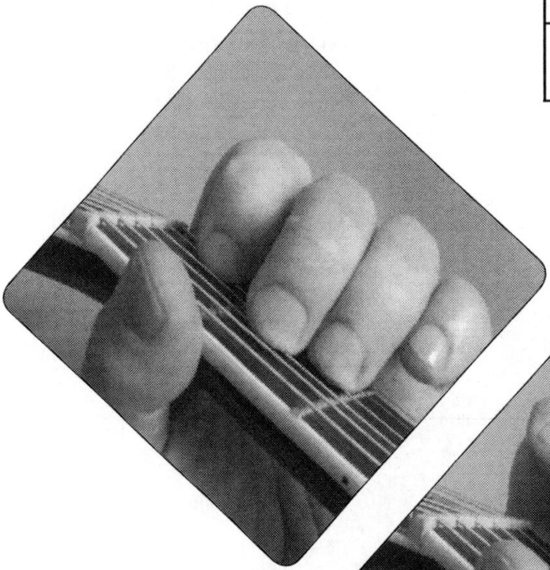

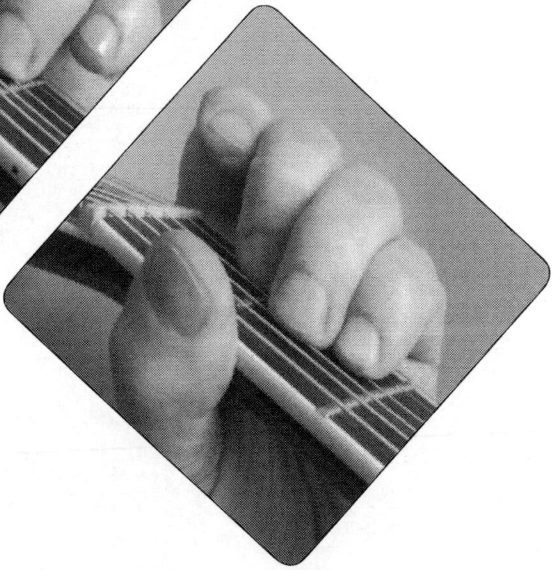

Now do Am chord again with 2nd 3rd and 4th fingers, as in the barre chord position.

# STEP 3

Now lower your thumb to the middle of the guitar neck. And at the very same time, add your 1st finger across and outside the nut.

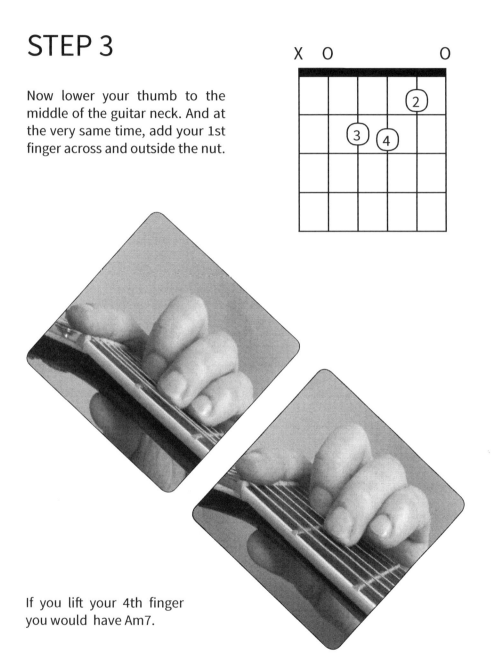

If you lift your 4th finger you would have Am7.

From Am7 add your 4th finger on 2nd string 2nd fret - This is A7.

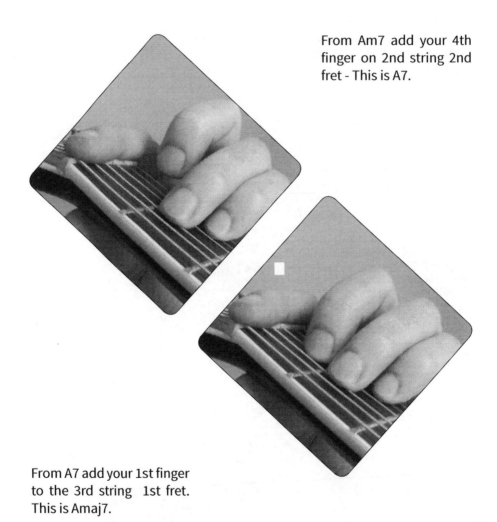

From A7 add your 1st finger to the 3rd string   1st fret. This is Amaj7.

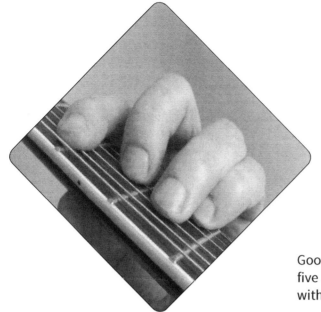

From here slide up two frets. This gives you Bmaj7.

Good guitarists bar across five strings and mute the 6th with the fingertip.

For open chords *(Except E's)* the 6th string is muted with the thumb. But because your thumb is now low and centred it cannot mute the 6th string.

Instead it is done with the 1st fingertip. The 7th fret is the exception. These are all E type chords an open 6th string (E) complements them.

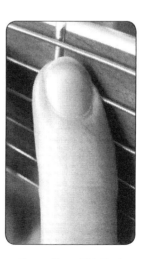

Exception - 7th Fret

# PLAYING TIP

Most top guitarists have what looks like a *Double Jointed 3rd Finger*. It means they can play A shaped barre chords with the 1st and 3rd fingers only.

- With three fingers you quickly run out of space as you move up the guitar neck

- With a double jointed 3rd finger, you can keep moving this very important chord shape up the fretboard.

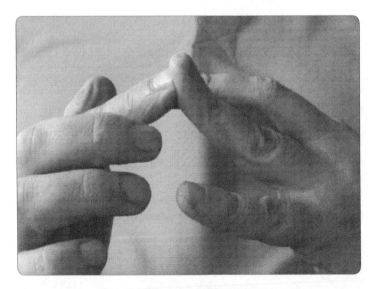

Bend It Back

Nobody is born with this skill - *But It Can Be Developed*. Bend your *3rd Finger* back *(Chord Hand)* as shown here a few times every day. After a few weeks you should be able to play chords with it.

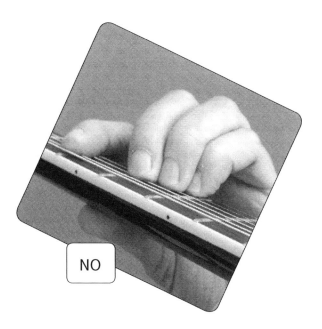

NO

Trying to play barre chords, with a barre finger and the other three fingers in one fret, closes doors. As well as being quite difficult to quickly change into, you run out of space for your fingers once you move past the third fret.

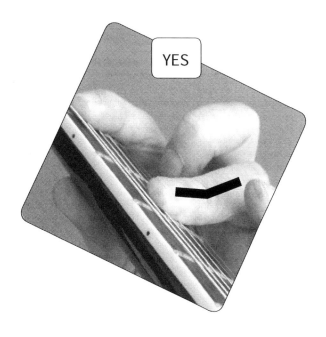

YES

# D

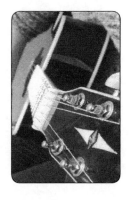

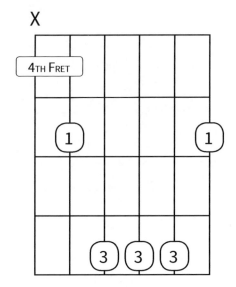

X

4TH FRET

① ①

③ ③ ③

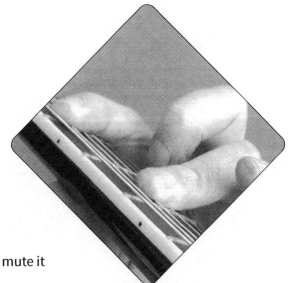

1st fingertip *Touching* 6th string to mute it

# E

O

| 6TH FRET | | | | |

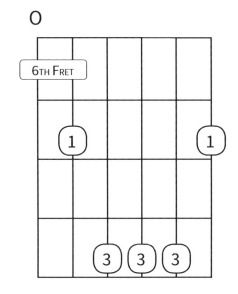

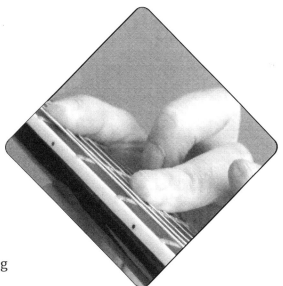

1st fingertip *NOT Touching* 6th string

# PRACTICE PROGRAM

# LESSON 16

- Practice Finger Exercise - *Page 86*
- Practice Strumming Some E Saped Bar Chords
- Practice Step 1 - *Page 165*
- Practice Step 2 - *Page 166*
- Practice Step 3 - *Page 167*

---

# NOTES

# LESSON 17

## HOW TO VAMP
## GUITAR RHYTHMS

# HOW TO VAMP
# GUITAR RHYTHMS

When moving from one bar chord to another, release the finger pressure and lightly slide your hand. Once you arrive at the next chord, apply pressure to the strings again. If you do not do this you will cramp very quickly.

Cramping is also caused by strumming bar chords and trying to keep your fingers constantly held down. Decreasing and increasing your hand / finger pressure *(Vamping)* during a strum pattern sounds better, gives your hand a rest, and gives variety to rhythms.

Fingers *Lightly* Touching Strings

- When you *Vamp* a chord
- When you *Slide Up And Down* the guitar neck

# MUTE

You can vamp with both the rhythm and chord hand.

Here we will look at two ways of practicing this invaluable technique with your chord hand.

- *Lightly* touch the strings
- *DO NOT* press strings down during the strum

# VAMP

- Fingers *Press Strings Down* during the strum
- Then they *Lift Off* but remain lightly touching the strings

Be very careful though. This is more difficult to do than it looks. But if you practice very slowly, you should soon perfect vamping. As well as making rhythms sound much more interesting, there is also less chance of getting cramp in your hand.

# VAMPING
# IN RHYTHMS

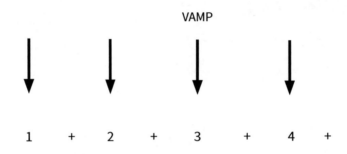

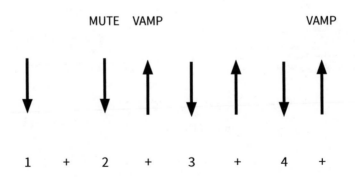

# 3 MORE EXAMPLES

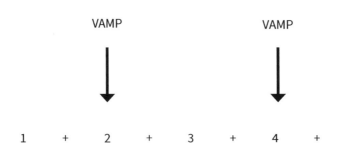

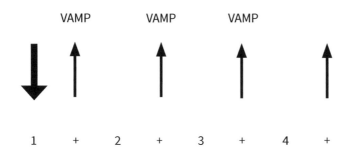

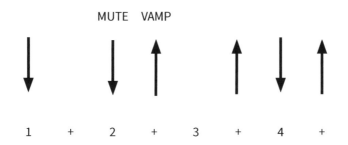

# PRACTICE PROGRAM

# LESSON 17

- Practice Finger Exercise - *Page 86*

- Practice Vamping - *Page 178*

- Practice Bending Your 3rd Finger - *Page 170*

- Practice Strumming Some A Shaped Bar Chords

- Reread How Not To Learn Guitar - *Page 10*

---

# NOTES

# LESSON 18

## 8

### MOST PLAYED
### GUITAR RHYTHMS

# 8 MOST PLAYED GUITAR RHYTHMS

### RHYTHM 1

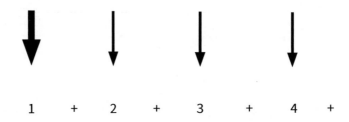

### RHYTHM 2

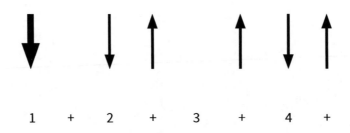

## RHYTHM 3

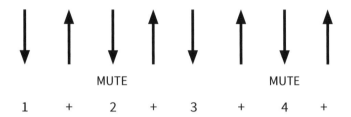

|   | | | | | | | | |
|---|---|---|---|---|---|---|---|---|
|   | | MUTE | | | | MUTE | | |
| 1 | + | 2 | + | 3 | + | 4 | + | |

## RHYTHM 4

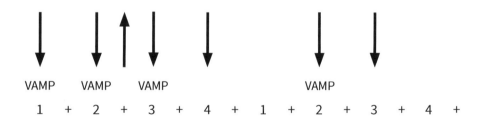

| VAMP | | VAMP | | VAMP | | | | | | VAMP | | | | | |
|------|---|------|---|------|---|---|---|---|---|------|---|---|---|---|---|
| 1 | + | 2 | + | 3 | + | 4 | + | 1 | + | 2 | + | 3 | + | 4 | + |

## RHYTHM 5

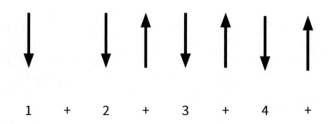

## RHYTHM 6

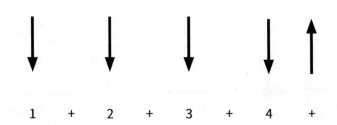

## RHYTHM 7

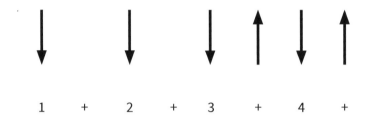

## RHYTHM 8

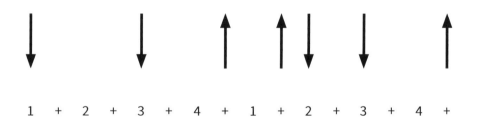

# PRACTICE PROGRAM

# LESSON 18

- Practice Finger Exercise - *Page 86*
- Review Rolling - *Page 52*
- Practice Not More Than 3 Rhythms At A Time
- Practice Strumming E and A Shaped Bar Chords

---

# NOTES

# LESSON 19

How To Adjust A Guitar Neck

How To Take Off A String

How To Put On A String

How To Tune Your Guitar
After Changing Strings

# HOW TO ADJUST A GUITAR NECK

All guitar necks are subject to stress, mainly from the strings. However, it can also be caused by sudden changes in weather conditions. Most guitars now have a rod with an adjustable nut in the neck. As well as letting you make adjustments it also helps to strengthen it.

Sometimes a guitar neck might become slightly bowed, humped or warped. This makes it more difficult to play. Also it will not sound quite right. The following guidelines should help you to correct it.

- Hold guitar up *To Eye Level*
- Look along *Both Edges* of fretboard
- Loosen 3rd and 4th strings slightly
- Remove nut cover (If there is one)
- Fit right sized allen key in the nut
- Turn it *Very Gently*
  (a fraction of a turn at a time)

Turn *Up* To Loosen
*Raises* The Strings

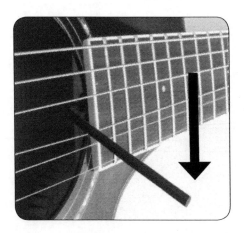

Turn *Down* To Tighten
*Lowers* The Strings

Once it looks straight, you could give the nut a very slight turn to compensate for the extra tension that is added when the loose strings are tightened and tuned.

# HUMP

## In The Middle

*Loosen* The Nut

# BOW

## In The Middle

*Tighten* The Nut

The truss rod can also be found in the head of the guitar

# HOW TO
# TAKE OFF A STRING

Changing guitar strings is easy once you know what you're doing. A good
string winder will help greatly. As well as saving you a lot of time, it gives
a great finishing touch.

## STEP 1

- Attach the string winder to the tuning head

- Turn it a few times to loosen the string

# STEP 2

Slide the string winder
*Under* the bridge pin

# STEP 3

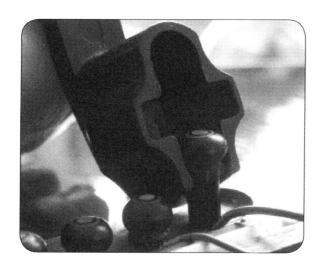

Gently push the pin
*Upwards* to remove
the string

# HOW TO
# PUT ON A STRING

## STEP 1

Push the string down *5 Centimetres*

Push the pin in *Lightly,* making sure the string is in the slot

## STEP 2

As you push and hold the pin down with your thumb, pull the string back up *(Quick Firm Pull)* until it *Locks Into Place*. This gives more security. If you don't snap the pins into place like this, they often pop back out when you try to tighten the strings.

# STEP 3

After threading the string through the tuning head, pull until it is about **12 Centimetres** out from the fretboard.

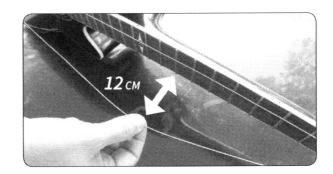

# STEP 4

For the last few turns, you may also have to *Press On The Pins* with the heel pad of your rhythm hand. This stops them from popping out.

Trap the string with your thumb. Start winding.

# STEP 5

Clip the strings for a *Neat Finish*

# HOW TO TUNE YOUR GUITAR

## AFTER CHANGING STRINGS

If you have just put on a new set of guitar strings, you now know that the job is not finished until they are tuned. A clip-on guitar tuner makes this much easier, especially if you're a beginner.

1   Place the heel pad of your hand on the bridge pins
    *(Helps to Stop The Pins From Popping Out as you tighten the strings)*

2   Slot the string winder over the tuning pegs with your other hand

3   Wind all strings reasonably tight

4   Switch on your guitar tuner

5   Tune the strings

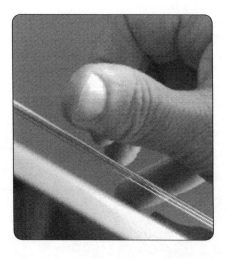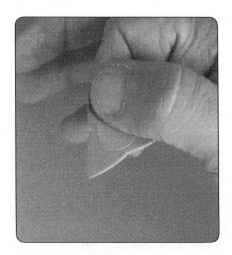

Pick strings with your thumb or a guitar pick

Heel pad on bridge pins to stop them popping out

# VERY IMPORTANT

Usually guitar strings would be in tune by now. But not this time. Because they are only on a few minutes, they need time to settle. Also the first three strings go out of tune because you tightened up the other three.

6   Tune all six strings two more times.

7   After that strum your guitar for about a minute.
    This helps to settle the strings.

8   Finally check each string again with the tuner.
    They should now stay in tune as you play.

# PRACTICE PROGRAM

# LESSON 19

- Practice Finger Exercise - *Page 86*
- Practice The Guitar Triangle - *Page 16*
- Practice The Magic Move - *Page 130*

---

# NOTES

# LESSON 20

## 50

### MOST PLAYED
### GUITAR CHORDS

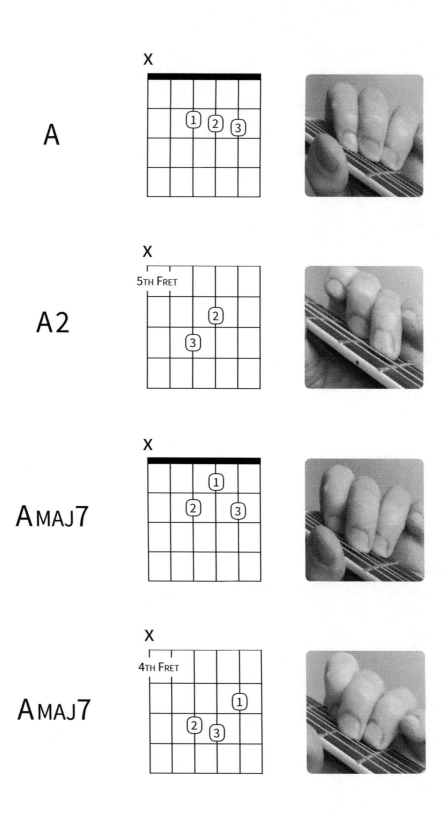

A

A2
5TH FRET

AMAJ7

AMAJ7
4TH FRET

**A**m

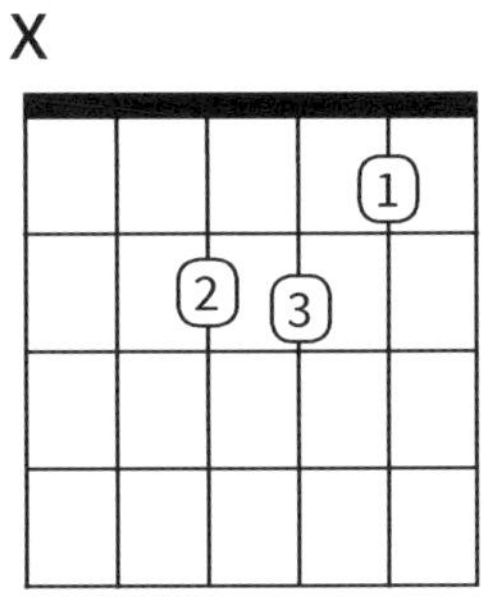

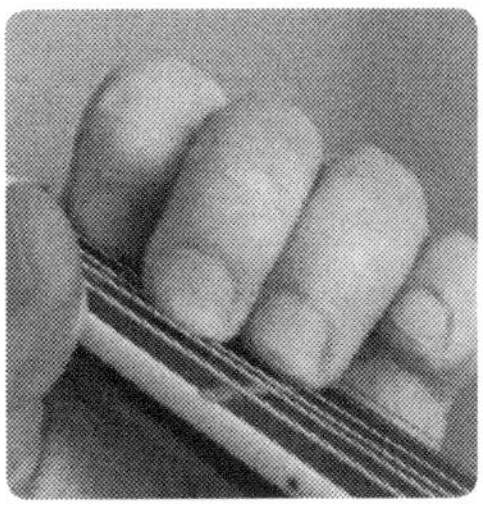

**A**m7

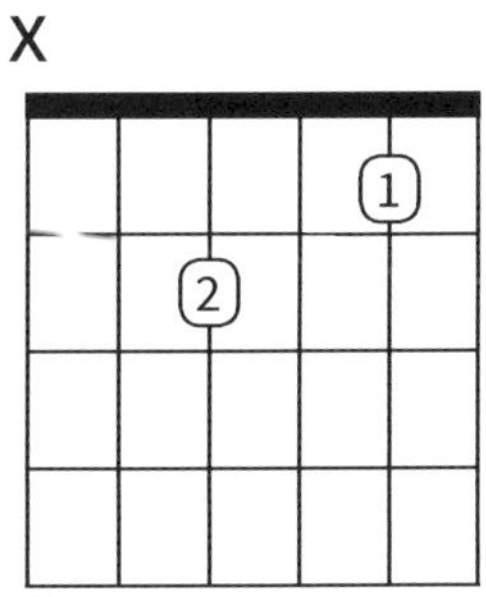

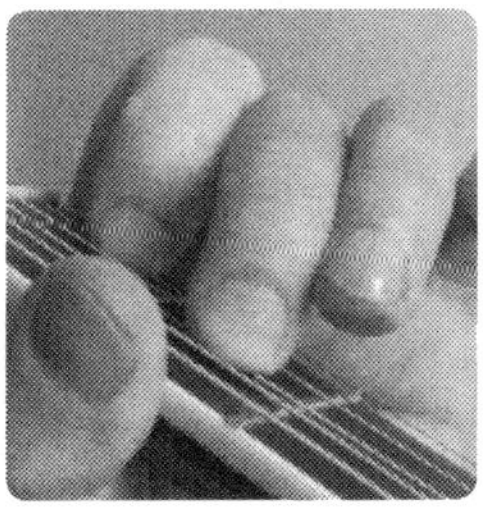

**A7**

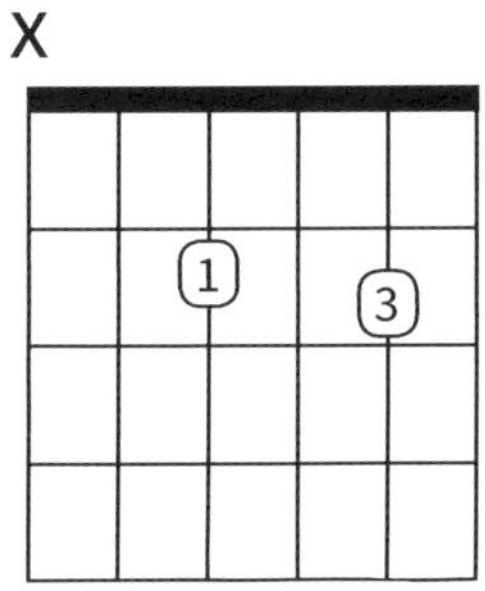

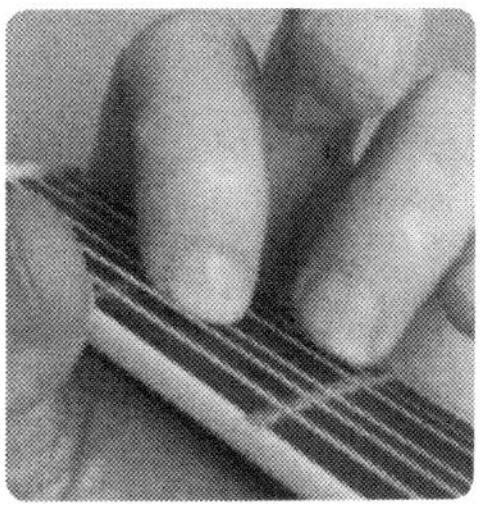

**A7**sus4

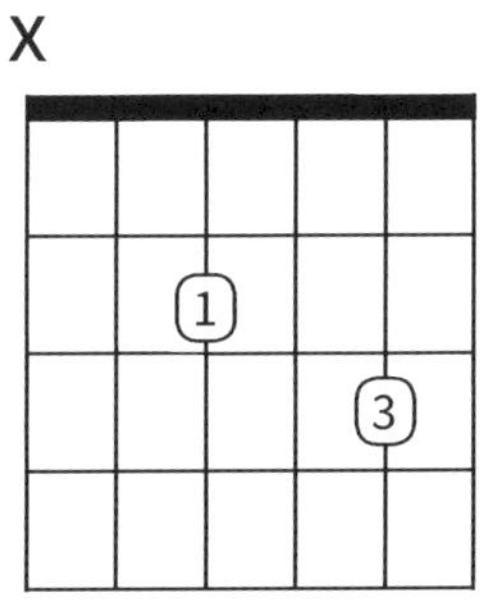

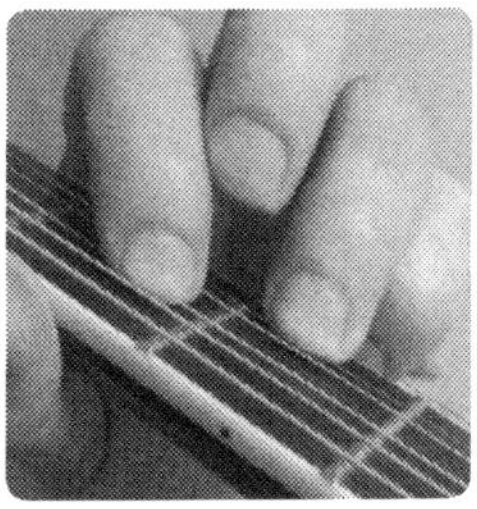

## A/E

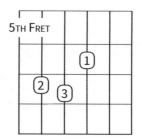

5TH FRET

## B

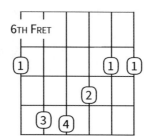

6TH FRET

## Bsus4

X

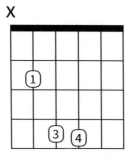

## BMAJ7

X

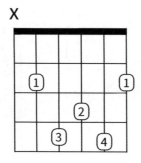

## B7

## Bm

## C

## C/G

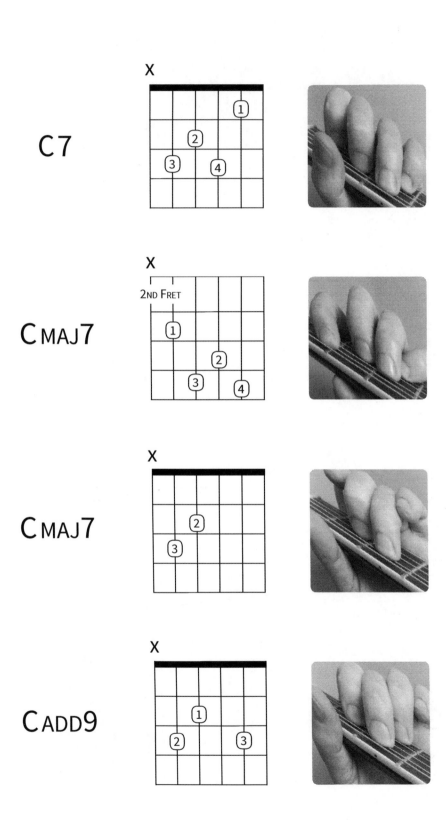

C7

CMAJ7

2ND FRET

CMAJ7

CADD9

**C/B**

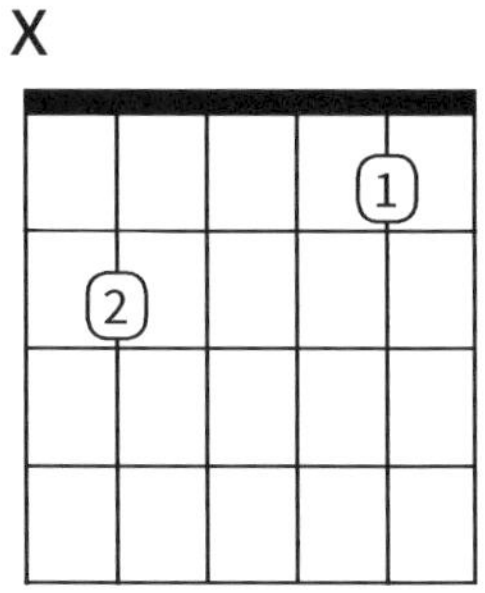

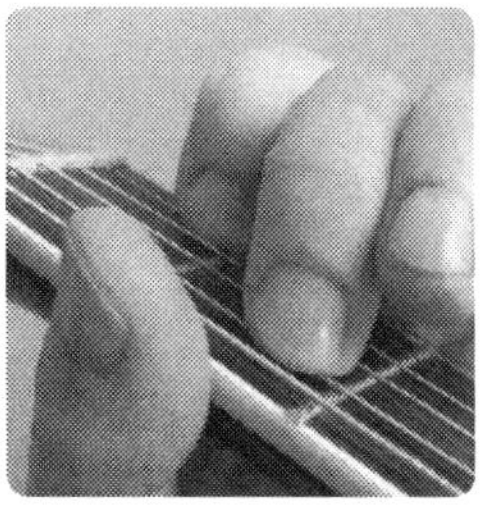

**D**

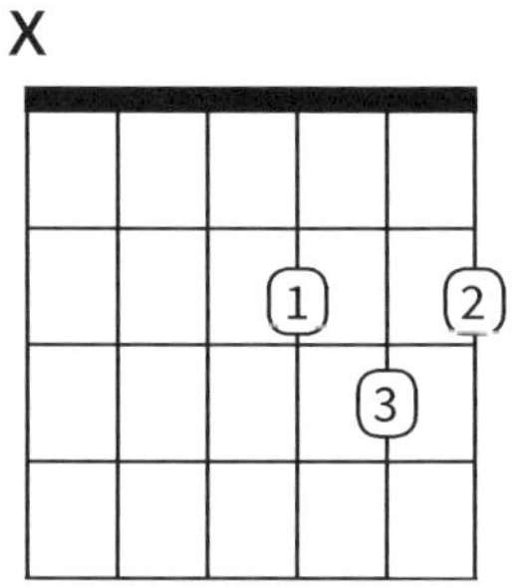

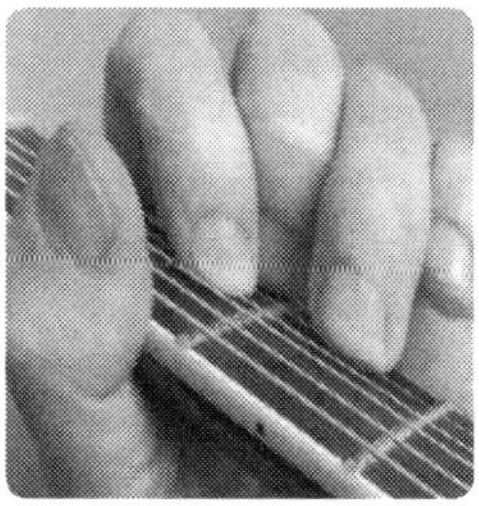

**Dм**

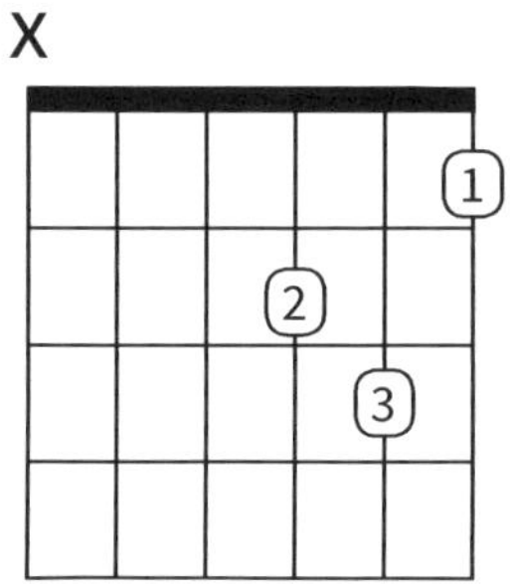

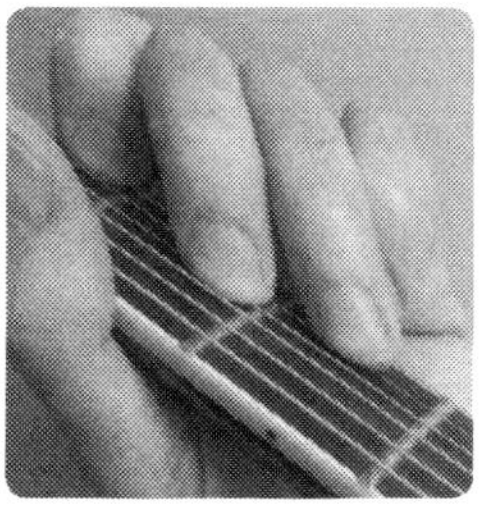

**Dм7**

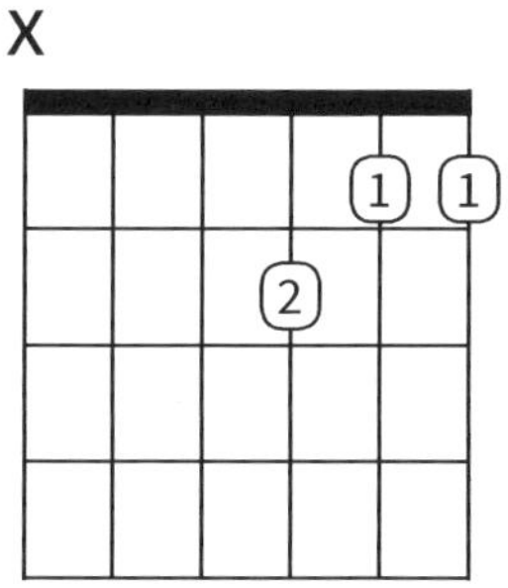

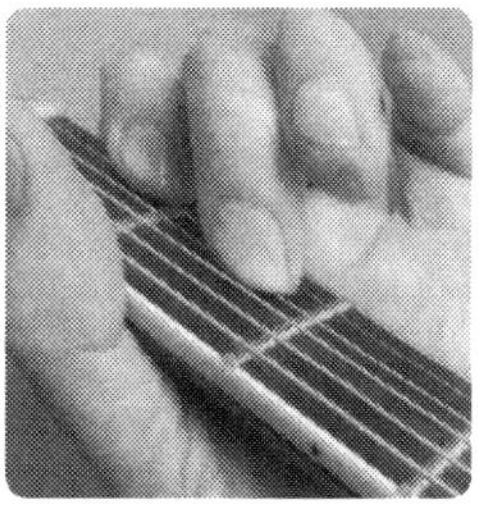

**D**MAJ7

**D**MAJ9

**D**2

**D**SUS4

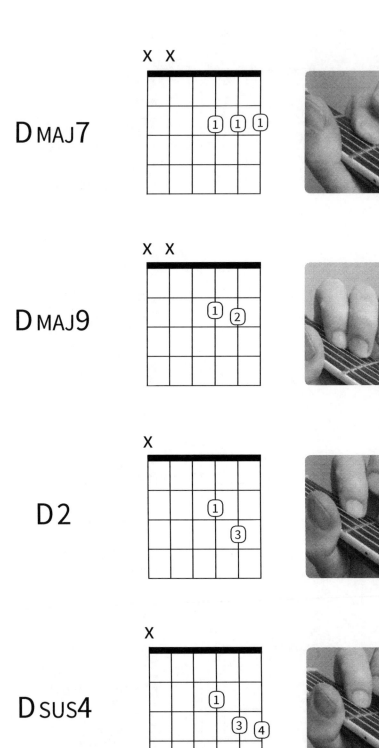

**E**

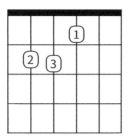 

**E7**

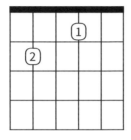 

**Em**

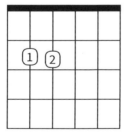 

**Em7**

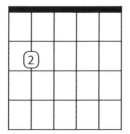 

**E**M7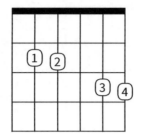

**E**M/G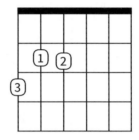

**E**MAJ7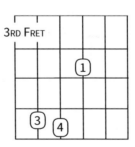

3RD FRET

**E**SUS4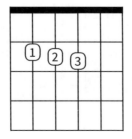

## F

PAGE 140-142

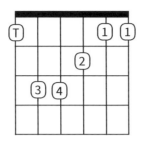 

## F2

PAGE 143

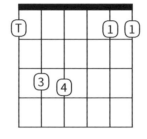 

## FMAJ7

x   x

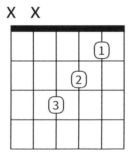 

## F#

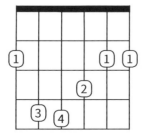 

F#m

F#m7

G

G

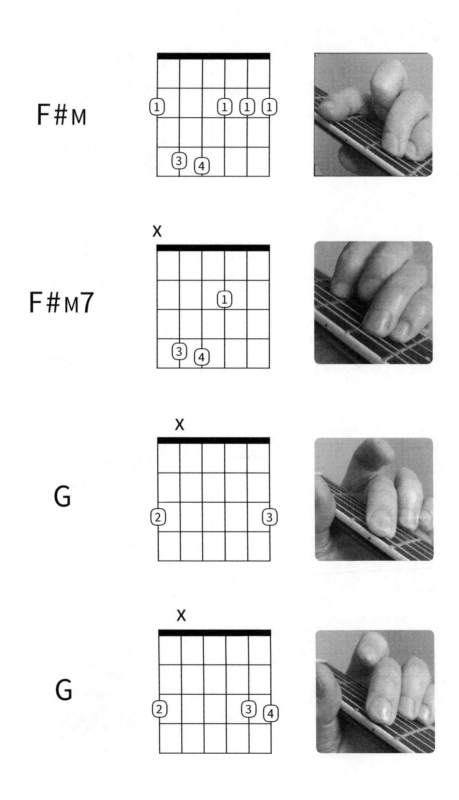

## G6

## G7

## Gmaj7

## Gaddc

# Gsus4

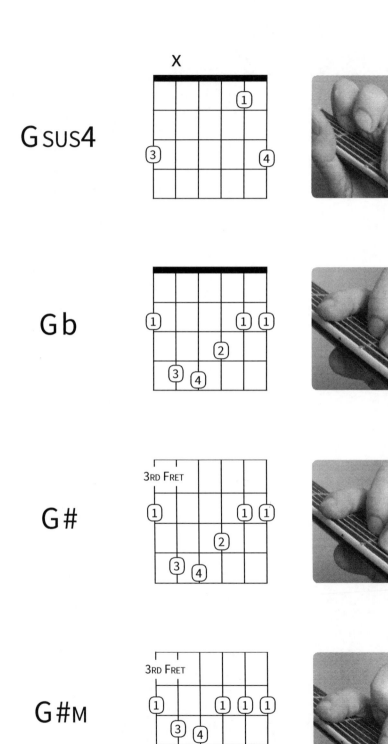

# Gb

# G#

# G#m

# CHORD INDEX

| | M | 7 | M7 | MAJ7 | 2 | SUS4 | 7SUS4 | 6 | MAJ9 | ADD9 | 7SUS2 | /E | MSUS4 | /B | /G |
|---|---|---|---|---|---|---|---|---|---|---|---|---|---|---|---|
| A | 198 | 108 | | 20 | 23 | 20 | | 199 | | | | 200 | | | |
| B | 162 | 201 | 201 | 200 | | 200 | | | | | | | 71 | | |
| C | 128 | | | 106 | | | | | 92 | | | | | 203 | 201 |
| D | 93 | 203 | | 143 | 24 | 22 | 204 | | 20 | | 23 | 107 | | | |
| E | 109 | 68 | 24 | 22 | | 206 | 69 | | | | | | | | |
| F | 140 | | | 129 | 207 | | | | | | | | | | |
| F# | 159 | 160 | | 208 | | | | | | | | | | | |
| G | 124 | | 209 | 24 | | 210 | | 21 | | | | | | | |

# ABOUT THE AUTHOR

Author of 3 Amazon #1 Best Sellers, Pauric Mather is from Dublin, Ireland. A professional guitarist since 1987 he has played with many successful artists.

He is also a leading expert in guitar teaching and one of the very few to have achieved outstanding success as a performer, writer, and guitar teacher.

Writing a guitar book - 2009

Finbar Furey & Pauric Mather - 1997

Antonio De Torres *(1817 - 1892)* built the first acoustic guitar in Almería, Spain around 1850.

Pauric Mather - 2016

Pauric Mather's ground breaking guitar books and playing lessons are truly unique. Easily the most individual & personalised you will ever find.

What's even more remarkable is that you need no knowledge of music to learn from his teaching style.

HomeGuitarAcademy.com